DEDICATED BY ESPECIAL PERMISS

HER MAJESTY THE

THE

WIVES OF ENGLAND,

THEIR

RELATIVE DUTIES,

DOMESTIC INFLUENCE, AND SOCIAL OBLIGATIONS

Sarah (Stickney)

BY MRS. ELLIS,

AUTHOR OF "THE WOMEN OF ENGLAND," "THE DAUGHTERS OF ENGLAND,"
"THE POETRY OF LIFE," ETC.

" The greatest difficulty of my task has been the laying bare, as it were, before the public eye, the privacy of married life—of that life whose sorrows the heart alone can know, and with whose joys it is the universal privilege of all who share them, that no stranger shall intermeddle.
" But if the principles it has been my simple aim to advocate, should meet the approbation of my countrywomen, I would fondly hope to be associated with their fireside enjoyments, as one whose highest ambition would have been to render their pleasures more enduring, their hopes more elevated, and their happiness more secure."—*From the Author's Preface.*

AUTHOR'S EDITION,

COMPLETE IN ONE VOLUME.

NEW YORK:

J. & H. G. LANGLEY, 57 CHATHAM-STREET.
1843.

TO HER MAJESTY THE QUEEN,

IN WHOSE EXALTED STATION

THE SOCIAL VIRTUES OF DOMESTIC LIFE PRESENT THE BRIGHTEST EXAMPLE

TO HER COUNTRYWOMEN,

AND THE SUREST PRESAGE OF HER EMPIRE'S GLORY;

𝕿𝖍𝖎𝖘 𝖁𝖔𝖑𝖚𝖒𝖊 𝖎𝖘 𝖌𝖗𝖆𝖙𝖊𝖋𝖚𝖑𝖑𝖞 𝕴𝖓𝖘𝖈𝖗𝖎𝖇𝖊𝖉,

BY HER MAJESTY'S

MOST OBEDIENT AND MOST DEVOTED SERVANT,

THE AUTHOR.

PREFACE.

In writing on any subject, and particularly for the purpose of doing good, there are always two extremes to be avoided—that of being too general, and that of being too minute.

By generalizing too much, the writer incurs the risk of being considered by the reader as having little actual knowledge of the state of human affairs, and consequently little sympathy either with those who enjoy, or with those who suffer. Without saying any thing to disparage in other respects the value of those excellent books on female duty, in many of which are included the duties of married women, I confess they have all appeared to me too general—too much as if the writer had not been personally identified with the subject, had never entered into the minutiæ of private and domestic life, or did not feel, what the heart of woman must feel, under its peculiar trials.

But, while endeavoring to avoid this extreme, I am quite alive to the suspicion that I may have fallen into the other; and if the mere ambition of writing a book had been my object, I should have felt painfully that those who read only for amusement might lay aside the volume altogether, as trifling, common-place, and tame. Yet such is my confidence in the power of human sympathy, that I fearlessly trust the practical hints which occupy these pages to the kindness of my countrywomen, assuring them that I ask for no higher reward, than, that while some of them are reading my homely details of familiar things, they should feel that in the writer they have found a sister and a friend,—one who is bound to the same heritage with themselves, sharing the same lot, and while struggling under much weakness of resolution, and many disadvantages of heart and character, is subject to the same hopes, and the same fears, both as regards this life and the next.

The greatest difficulty of my task, however, has been to me the laying bare, as it were, before the public eye, the privacy of married life—of that life whose sorrows the heart alone can know, and with whose joys it is the universal privilege of all who share them, that no stranger shall intermeddle. This difficulty, of the extent of which I was not fully aware before commencing the work, has sometimes thrown a hesitancy —I had almost said a delicacy—in the way of writing with the strength which the occasion demanded ; and I could not but feel that the subject itself was one better calculated for confidential fireside intercourse, than for a printed volume.

But if then the principles it has been my simple aim to advocate, should meet the approbation of my countrywomen, I would fondly hope to be associated with their fireside enjoyments as one whose highest earthly ambition would have been to render their pleasures more enduring, their hopes more elevated, and their happiness more secure.

Rose Hill, February 16th, 1843.

WIVES OF ENGLAND.

CHAPTER I.

THOUGHTS BEFORE MARRIAGE.

In commencing a work addressed particularly to married women, it might appear a little out of place to devote a whole chapter to the subject of "thoughts before marriage," did not the writer suppose it probable, that if married women should deem the following pages worthy of their notice, those who are about to assume the responsibility of wives, might feel equally curious to ascertain the nature of their contents. In this chapter, then, I would venture to recommend a few inquiries to those who have not yet passed the Rubicon, and with whom, therefore, it may not be too late to retract, if they should find they have not correctly calculated the consequences of the step they are about to take; or, what is still more probable, if they have not coolly and impartially estimated their own capability for rendering it one of prudence and safety both to themselves and others. On the other hand, the inquiries I would propose, are such as, where the mind and character are fitly prepared for this important change, will tend to confirm the best resolutions; while they will assist in detecting every latent evil which might otherwise lie in wait, to rise up after the season of deliberation is past, like clouds in the horizon, which gradually spread their gloom across the sky, and finally obscure the sunshine of every future day.

The great object to be aimed at by all women about to enter upon the married state, is to examine calmly and dispassionately the requirements of this state; to put away all personal feeling; and to be not only willing, but determined, to look the subject fairly in the face, and to see its practical bearing upon the interest and the happiness of those with whom they may be associated.

Perhaps there never yet was a woman of warm feelings, or man either, who had not, in early life, some vision of conjugal felicity, which after experience and knowledge of the world have failed to stamp with the impress of reality. Some, believing themselves capable of contributing their share to this measure of earthly happiness, and disappointed in not finding an equal companion, have wisely declined entering upon the married state altogether; while others, more confident of success, have made the experiment for themselves, believing, that though all the world may have failed in realizing their dreams of bliss, they and theirs will be fortunate enough to exhibit to the wonder of mankind, an instance of perfect connubial happiness.

It is needless to decide which of these two parties deserve the highest meed of commendation for their prudence and common sense. But it is equally needless to belong to either class of individuals. "What!" exclaims the young enthusiast, "shall we not even *hope* to be happy?" Yes. Let us hope as long as we can; but let it be in subservience to reason and to truth. Let us hope only to be happy ourselves, so long as we make others happy too; and let us expect no measure of felicity beyond what this world has afforded to those who were wiser and better than we are.

"But why then," exclaims the same enthusiast, "all the fine talk we hear about marriage? and why, in all the stories we read, is marriage made the end of woman's existence?" Ah! there lies the evil. Marriage, like death, is too often looked upon as the *end;* whereas both are but the beginning of states of existence infinitely more important than that by which they were preceded; yet each taking from that their tone and character, and each proportioned in their enjoyment to the previous preparation which has been made for their happiness or misery.

The education of young ladies is too frequently such as to lead them naturally to suppose, that all the training, and all the discipline they undergo, has reference only to this *end.* The first evidence that marriage is thus regarded by many young women, is seen in a petulant rebellion against the restraints of home, and the requirements of parental authority, accompanied by a threat, not always distinctly uttered, that the first opportunity of escaping from domestic thraldom shall not be neglected. This species of rebellion against rightful authority, is much cherished by school-companions and sisters; while the gossip of servants, to whom the indignant sufferers sometimes appeal, and the general tenor of what is called light reading, tend to keep up the same kind of spirited determination to rush upon the uncertainties of marriage, in the hope of escaping from the certainties of home. A polite and flattering lover next presents himself. The persecuted or neglected damsel finds at last that her merits are appreciated, and while the gates of an imaginary Eden are still open, she enters eagerly among its fruits and flowers, never stopping to inquire if

" The trail of the serpent is over them still."

Such is the natural history of one half at least of those early marriages, which fix the doom of women for this world, and sometimes for the next. What wonder, then, that a sincere and earnest friend, and an affectionate well-wisher of her sex, should deem it necessary, even on the near approach of that day which is generally spoken of as making two human beings happy, to request

the weaker, and consequently the more easily deluded party, to pause and think again.

Although I am one of the last persons who could wish to introduce in any plausible form, to an upright and honorable mind, the bare idea of the possibility of breaking an engagement; yet as there are cases in which an engagement of marriage, if literally kept, must necessarily be violated in spirit, I cannot help thinking, that of two evils, it is, in this case, especially desirable to choose the least; and to prefer inflicting a temporary pain, and enduring an inevitable disgrace, to being the means of destroying the happiness of a lifetime, with the self-imposed accompaniment of endless remorse.

In the first place, then, I would ask, are you about to bring to the altar, and to offer, in the sight of God, a faithful and devoted heart? To answer with a mere expression of belief, is not sufficient here. There must be certainty on this point, if not on any other. There are many tests by which this important fact may be ascertained, and of these I shall particularize a few. The first is, whom are you loving?—the man who stands before you with all his "imperfections on his head"—his faults of temper, follies, inconsistencies, and past misdeeds? Is this the man you love? or is it some ideal and perfect being whom you will fail to recognise in the husband of your after life? If the latter case be yours, go back, and wait, for your acquaintance has yet to be formed on the only sure basis—that of honesty and truth; and you might as safely unite yourself with a being you had never seen before, as with one whom you had seen without having known or understood.

The discovery that you have mistaken the real character of your lover, need not, however, be any barrier to the ultimate fulfilment of your engagement with him. All that you have to do, is to wait until you have studied his real character, and ascertained that you can still love him, though you no longer believe him to be without a fault.

During the progress of this study, the delay it will necessarily occasion, may be made to answer two valuable ends; for at the same time that you have been deceived, it is more than probable that you have been deceiving. Not intentionally, perhaps, yet the effect may be as calamitous as if you had designedly practised upon the partial credulity of your lover. It is of the utmost importance, then, that you inquire into the nature of your own conduct, not only towards him, but towards others in his presence. Have you, during the season of courtship, been acting a part which you never before sustained, or which you do not intend to sustain as a wife? Have you been more amiable to your admirer, than you expect to be to your husband? If you have, there are two ways of remedying this evil, for an evil it certainly is; and one of these you are bound in common honesty to adopt: you must either defer your marriage until your real character has been brought to light, and clearly understood; or, you must determine, from this time forward, by the Divine blessing on your endeavors, that you will be in reality the amiable being you have appeared.

And now, having learned to see your lover as he is, I would ask again, whether you are quite sure that your affections are entirely and irrevocably his. If on this point there is doubt, there must be danger; but still there are tests to be applied, which may in some measure reduce those doubts to certainty. The most important question, in a case of doubt, is, whether your heart lingers after any other object; and this may be best ascertained by asking yourself still further, whether there is any other man in the world, of whom it would give you pain to hear that he was likely to be married. If there is not, you are in all probability safe in this respect, and yet you may not love the man you are about to marry, as he hopes, deserves, and believes himself to be loved. I would ask, then, are you weary of his presence, and relieved when he goes away? or are you disposed to exercise less charity and forbearance towards his faults, than towards the faults of others? for if his failings annoy and irritate you more than those of men in general, depend upon it, you do not love him as you ought. If, too, you feel ashamed of him before marriage, there is little probability that you will afterwards evince towards him that respect and reverence which is right and seemly in a wife.

In order to ascertain these points clearly, it is good for every woman before she marries, to see the man of her choice in the company of her friends, and especially to see him associated and compared with those whose opinion she esteems most highly. We are all more or less influenced by the secret sympathies of our common nature. In nothing can we think or feel alone; and few cases show more plainly the weakness and liability to delusion under which we labor, than the strong confidence we sometimes entertain in the correctness of our own judgment, until some new trial is made; and then immediately, as if by a kind of instinct, placing ourselves in the situation of others, we see as it were with their eyes, think with their thoughts, and arrive at their conclusions. This tendency of our nature is often discovered in the reading of books, which we have both enjoyed and admired alone; but no sooner do we read them in company with a critical friend, than we see at once their defects, and can even use against them the same powers of criticism ourselves. Happy is it for those whose judgment, thus influenced, is confined in its exercise to books!—happy for them if they never know what it is to find the talents and the recommendations of a lover disappear in a moment, on the approach of an interesting and influential friend, and disappear in such a way as never to be recalled again!

Yet, having stood this test, it is still possible to doubt, and, without sufficient love, your engagement may still be only just dragged on, because you have no sufficient plea for breaking it off. You may perhaps esteem your lover highly; you may feel grateful for his kindness, and flattered by his admiration; you may also feel a strong desire to make him the happy man he believes he can be with you, and you alone—you may feel all this, and yet, I repeat, you may not love him as a woman ought to love her husband. This will be more clearly proved by an increase of sadness on your part, as the time of your marriage draws near, an indefinite apprehension that with you the pleasures of life are at an end, and a determination, requiring often to be renewed, that at least you will do your duty to one who deserves every thing from you.

Let me, however, ask what this duty is? It is not merely to serve him ; a hired menial could do that. The duty of a wife is what no woman ever yet was able to render without affection ; and it is therefore the height of presumption to think that you can coldly fulfil a duty, the very spirit of which is that of love itself.

It is possible, however, that you may still be mistaken. It is possible that the gradual opening of your eyes from the visions of girlish romance, which are apt to flit before the imaginative and inexperienced, may have given you a distaste both for your companion, and your future lot. If this be the case, the difficulty will be easily overcome by the exercise of a little good feeling and common sense. But in order to prove that this is really all, put this question to yourself—if you were quite sure there was some other woman as amiable, or more so, than you, with whom your friend could be equally happy, would you feel pleasure in his cultivating her acquaintance instead of yours?

If you can answer this question in the negative, you may yet be safe ; if not, the case is too decided to admit of a moment's hesitation. Your own integrity, and a sense of justice towards your friend, equally dictate the propriety of making him acquainted with the painful, the humiliating fact, that you do not love him ; and no man, after being convinced of this, could desire the fulfilment of a mere nominal engagement.

I am aware that the opinion of the world and the general voice of society are against such conduct, even where love is wanting ; and I am equally aware, that no woman ought to venture upon breaking an engagement on such grounds, without feeling her-self humbled to the very dust ; but I am not the less convinced, that it is the only safe, the only just line of conduct which remains to her who finds herself thus circumstanced, and that it is in reality more generous to her lover, than if she kept " the word of promise to his ear, and broke it to his hope."

But there may be other causes besides this, why an engagement should not be fulfilled. There may be a want of love on the part of your friend, or there may be instances of unfaithfulness too glaring to be overlooked ; and here let it be observed, that woman's love may grow after marriage—man's, never. If, therefore, he is indifferent or unfaithful as a lover, what must be expected of him as a husband?

It is one of the greatest misfortunes to which women are liable, that they cannot, consistently with female delicacy, cultivate, before an engagement is made, an acquaintance sufficiently intimate to lead to the discovery of certain facts which would at once decide the point, whether it was prudent to proceed further towards taking that step, which is universally acknowledged to be the most important in a woman's life.

One of these facts, which can only be ascertained on a close acquaintance, is the tendency there is in some individuals to overawe, and keep others at a distance. Now, if on the near approach of marriage, a woman finds this tendency in the companion she has chosen, if she cannot open to him her whole heart, or if he does not open his heart to her, but maintains a distant kind of authoritative manner, which shuts her out from sympathy and equality with himself, it is time for her to pause, and think seriously before she binds herself for life to that *worst of all slavery*, the fear of a husband. I have no scruple in using this expression, because where the connection is so intimate, and the sphere of action necessarily so confined, if fear usurps the place of confidence and love, it must naturally engender a servile disposition to deceive, either by falsehood or evasion, wherever blame would attach to a full disclosure of the truth.

I have already said that it is a prudent plan for the woman who intends to marry, to try the merits of her lover, or rather her own estimate of them, by allowing him an opportunity of associating with her friends. Such precautionary measures, however, are not easily carried out, except at some sacrifice of delicate and generous feeling; and, generally speaking, the less a woman allows her name to be associated with that of her husband before marriage, the better. It is sometimes argued that an engagement entered into with right feelings, is of so binding and sacred a nature, that persons thus related to each other, may be seen together, both in public and private, almost as if they were really married; and to such it may appear a cold kind of caution still to say "beware!" Yet such is the uncertain nature of all human affairs, that we need not look far for instances of the most improbable changes taking place, after all possibility of change had been banished from our thoughts. Within a month, a week, nay, even a day, of marriage, there have been discoveries made which have fully justified an entire disunion of the parties thus associated; and then how much better has it been, where their names had not been previously united, and where their appearance together had not impressed the idea of indissoluble connection upon the minds of others!

One of the most justifiable, and at the same time one of the most melancholy causes for such disunion, is the discovery of symptoms of insanity. Even a highly excited and disordered state of the nervous system, will operate with a prudent woman against an alliance of this nature. Yet here again, it is particularly unfortunate, that in cases of nervous derangement, the discovery is seldom fully made except in the progress of that close intimacy which immediately precedes marriage, and which consequently assumes the character of an indissoluble engagement. Symptoms of this nature, however, when exhibited in the conduct of a man, are of the most serious and alarming character. A woman laboring under such maladies, in their milder form, may be so influenced by authority as to be kept from doing any very extensive harm; but when a man, with the reins of government in his hand, loses the power to guide them, when his mind becomes the victim of morbid feeling, and his energies sink under imaginary burdens, there is no calculating the extent of calamity which may result to the woman who would be rash enough to link her destiny with his.

Another justifiable reason for setting aside an engagement of marriage, or protracting the fulfilment of it, is a failure of health, especially when either this, or the kind of malady already noticed, induces an incapacity for business, and for the duties which generally devolve upon the master of a household. It is true, that in cases where the individual thus afflicted does not himself see the propriety of withdrawing from the engagement, the hard, and apparently selfish part a woman has to act on these occasions is such as, in addition to her own sufferings, will probably bring upon her the blame of many who do not, and who cannot, understand the case; and the more delicate her feelings are towards the friend she is thus compelled to treat with apparent harshness, the less likely she will be to exculpate herself by an exposure to the world of his inconsistency, or his weakness. Thus, as in many of the acts of woman's life, she has to be the sufferer every way; but still that suffering is less to every one concerned, than if she plunged herself into all the lamentable consequences of a union with a man who wanted either the mental or the physical capacity to keep her and hers from poverty and distress. In the former case, she will have the dictates of prudence and of conscience in her favor. In both, the world will be lavish of its blame; but in the latter only, could her portion be that of self-condemnation, added to irremediable misery.

After all these considerations have been duly weighed, and every test of truth and constancy applied to your affection for the object of your choice, there may yet remain considerations of infinite moment as they relate to your own fitness for entering upon the married state.

In the first place, what is it you are expecting?—to be always flattered? Depend upon it, if your faults were never brought to light before, they will be so now. Are you expecting to be always indulged? Depend upon it, if your temper was never tried before, it will be so now. Are you expecting to be always admired? Depend upon it, if you were never humble and insignificant before, you will have to be so now. Yes, you had better make up your mind at once to be uninteresting as long as you live, to all except the companion of your home; and well will it be for you, if you can always be interesting to him. You had better settle it in your calculations, that you will have to be crossed oftener than the day; and the part of wisdom will dictate, that if you persist in your determination to be married, you shall not only be satisfied, but cheerful to have these things so.

One important truth sufficiently impressed upon your mind will materially assist in this desirable consummation—it is the superiority of your husband, simply as a man. It is quite possible you may have more talent, with higher attainments, and you may also have been generally more admired; but this has nothing whatever to do with your position as a woman, which is, and must be, inferior to his as a man. For want of a satisfactory settlement of this point before marriage, how many disputes and misunderstandings have ensued, filling, as with the elements of discord and strife, that world of existence which ought to be a smiling Eden of perpetual flowers—not of flowers which never fade; but of flowers which, if they must die, neither droop nor wither from the canker in their own bosoms, or the worm which lies at their own roots.

It is a favorite argument with untried youth, that all things will come right in the end, where there is a sufficiency of love; but is it enough for the subjection of a woman's will, that she should love her husband? Alas! observation and experience alike convince us, that love has been well represented as a wayward boy; and the alternate exhibitions of contradiction and fondness which are dictated by affection alone, though interesting enough before the nuptial knot is tied, are certainly not those features in the aspect of his domestic affairs, whose combination a prudent man would most desire.

It is to sound judgment then, and right principle, that we must look, with the blessing of the Bestower of these good gifts, for ability to make a husband happy—sound judgment to discern what is the place designed for him and for us, in the arrangements of an all-wise Providence—and right principle to bring down every selfish desire, and every rebellious thought, to a due subserviency in the general estimate we form of individual duty.

But supposing this point satisfactorily settled, and an earnest and prayerful determination entered into to be but a secondary being in the great business of conducting the general affairs of social life, there are a few things yet to be thought of, a few duties yet to be discharged, before the final step can properly be taken. In the warmth and enthusiasm of youthful feeling, few women look much beyond themselves in the calculations they make upon their married future. To be loved, and cherished, is all they appear solicitous to stipulate for, forgetting the many wants and wishes that will necessarily arise out of the connection they are about to form. It may not be out of place then to remind them, how essential it is to comfort in the married state, that there should have been beforehand a clear understanding, and a strict agreement, with regard both to the general style of living, and the friendships and associations to be afterwards maintained. All secret wishes and intentions on these subjects, concealed by one party from the fear of their being displeasing to the other, are ominous of future disaster; and, indeed, I would almost venture so far as to advise, that unless such preliminaries can be satisfactorily adjusted, the parties had better make up their minds to separate; for these causes of difference will be of such frequent occurrence, as to leave little prospect of domestic peace.

If, however, the companion of your future home should not be disposed to candor on these points, you will probably have opportunities of judging for yourself; and such means of forming your conclusions ought on no account to be neglected. You will probably, for instance, have opportunies of ascertaining whether he is one of those who place their chief happiness in what is called good living, or, in other words, in the pleasures of the table; and if in his estimation wine forms a prominent part of these enjoyments, let not the fear of the world's censure operate for one moment against your separating yourself from such a man. If this should seem a harsh and hasty conclusion, remember that the evils of a gross and self-indulgent habit are such as generally increase with the advance of years, and, as the natural spirits fail, and health becomes impaired, are liable to give rise to the most fatal maladies both of mind and body. If, then, there is danger and disgust to apprehend on the side of indulgence, it is on the other hand a hard and unthankful duty for the wife to be perpetually restraining the appetite of her husband, and preaching up the advantages of abstinence to the man she loves. Nor is it improbable, or of rare occurrence, that under such circumstances she should actually lose his affection, for men like not the constant imposition of restraint upon their wishes; and so much happier—so much more privileged is the situation of her who can safely minister to the desires of her husband, that I would recommend to every woman to choose the man who can with propriety be indulged, rather than him whose habits of self-gratification already require restraint.

As the time of your marriage draws near, you will naturally be led with ease and pleasure into that kind of unlimited confidence with the companion of your future lot, which forms in reality the great charm of married life. But even here a caution is required, for though all the future, as connected with your own experience, must belong to him, all the past must belong to others. Never, therefore, make it the subject of your confidential intercourse to relate the history of your former love affairs, if you have had any. It is bad taste to allude to them at all, but especially so under such circumstances; and although such details might serve to amuse for the moment, they would in all probability be remembered against you at some future time, when each day will be sufficiently darkened by its own passing clouds.

With regard to all your other love affairs then, let " by-gones be by-gones." It could do no good whatever for you to remember them; and the more you are dissociated from every other being of his own sex, the more will the mind of your husband dwell upon you with unalloyed satisfaction. On the other hand, let no ill-advised curiosity induce you to pry too narrowly into his past life as regards affairs of this nature. However close your inquiries, they may still be baffled by evasion; and if it be an important point with you, as many women profess to make it, to occupy an unsullied page in the affections of your husband, it is wiser and safer to take for granted this flattering fact, than to ask whether any other name has been written on that page before. In this case, as well as your own, both honor and delicacy would suggest the propriety of drawing a veil over the past. It is sufficient for the happiness of married life that you share together the present and the future.

With such a field for the interchange of mutual thought, there can surely be no want of interest in your conversation, for the arrangements to be made are so new to both, and consequently so fraught with importance, that parties thus circumstanced, are proverbially good company only to each other.

Amongst these arrangements, if the choice of a residence be permitted you, and especially if your own temper is not good, or your manners not conciliating, avoid, as far as you can do so with prudence, and without thwarting your husband's wishes, any very close contact with his nearest relatives. There are not wanting numerous instances in which the greatest intimacy and most familiar associations of this kind have been kept up with mutual benefit and satisfaction; but generally speaking it is a risk, and you may not yourself be sufficiently amiable to bear, with a meek and quiet spirit, the general oversight, and well-meant interference, which mothers and sisters naturally expect to maintain in the household of a son and a brother. These considerations, however, must of course give way to the wishes of the husband and his family, as it is of the utmost importance not to offend his relatives in the outset by any appearance of contradiction or self-will; and besides which, he and his friends will be better judges than you can be, of the general reasons for fixing your future residence.

And now, as the time draws near, are you quite sure that your means are sufficient to enable you to begin the world with independence and respectability? Perhaps you are not a judge, and if not, you have no right to think of becoming a wife; for young men in general have little opportunity of making themselves acquainted with household economy; and who then is to make those innumerable calculations upon which will depend, not only the right government of your establishment, but also your peace of mind, your integrity of character, and your influence for time and for eternity?

Oh! what a happy day would that be for Britain, whose morning should smile upon the making of a law for allowing no woman to marry until she had become an economist, thoroughly acquainted with the necessary expenses of a respectable mode of living, and able to calculate the requirements of comfort, in connection with all the probable contingencies of actual life. If such a law should be so cruel as to suspend for a year or more every approach to the hymeneal altar, it would, at least, be equally effectual in averting that bitter repentance with which so many look back to the hurried and thoughtless manner in which they rushed blindfold upon an untried fate, and only opened their eyes to behold their madness and folly, when it was too late to avert the fatal consequences.

As a proof how little young men in general are acquainted with these matters, I have heard many who fully calculated upon living in a genteel and comfortable style, declare that a hundred pounds was sufficient for the furnishing of a house. Thus a hundred pounds on one side, either saved, borrowed, or begged, and fifty on the other, are not unfrequently deemed an ample provision, with a salary of two hundred, to begin the world with. It is true the young man finds that salary barely sufficient for himself; but then, he hears and reads how much is saved under *good* female management, and he doubts not but his deficiencies will be more than made up by his wife. It is true the young lady, with her ill health, and music lessons, and change of air, costs her father at least fifty pounds per annum, but she does not see how she shall cost her husband any thing at all! Sweet soul! She needs so little, and really would be content with any thing in the world, so that she might but live with him. Nay, she who has never learned to wait upon herself, would almost do without a servant, so self-denying, so devoted is her love.

Thus the two hopeful parties reason, and should a parent or a friend advise delay, the simple fact of their having been engaged, having expected to be married, and having made up their minds, appear to furnish sufficient arguments why they should proceed in their career of rashness and of folly. Parents who are kindly disposed, will hardly see their children rush upon absolute want at the commencement of their married life. The mother therefore pleads, the father calculates, and by deferring some of his own payments, or by borrowing from a friend, he is enabled to spare a little more than was at first promised, though only as a loan.

And how is this small additional sum too frequently appropriated? To the purchase of luxuries which the parents of the newly married pair waited ten or twenty years before they thought of indulging themselves with; and those who have tried every expedient, and drained every creditable source, to gratify the wishes of their imprudent children, have to contemplate the heart-sickening spectacle of beholding them begin the world in a style superior to that which their own industry and exertion, persevered in through half a lifetime, has alone enabled them to attain.

Now, though the delicate young lady may think she has little to do with these things, the honest-hearted Englishwoman, especially the practical Christian, will find that it belongs peculiarly to her province to see that just and right principles are made the foundation of her character as the mistress of a house ; and in order to carry out these principles so as to make them effectual in their operation upon her fellow-beings, and acceptable in the sight of God, she must begin in time, and while the choice remains to her, to practise self-denial, even in that act which is most intimately connected with her present and future happiness.

If the attention to economy, and the right feeling with regard to integrity, which I have so earnestly recommended in the " Women," and the " Daughters of England," have been studied in early youth, she will need no caution on the subject of delaying her marriage until prudence shall point out the proper time for her settlement in life. She will know a holier, deeper kind of love than that which would plunge the object of it in irremediable difficulties for her sake ; and though he may be inexperienced and imprudent, she will feel it a sacred trust, to have committed to her the care of his character and circumstances in these important and momentous concerns.

Serious and right views on subjects of this nature, are so intimately connected with the reality of the Christian character, that it is difficult to imagine how a high profession of religion can exist in connection with the kind of wilful and selfish imprudence above described. One thing, however, is certain, that let a woman's religious profession be what it may, if she be rash and inconsiderate on the subject of marriage, consulting only her own gratification, and mistaking mere fondness for deep and enduring affection, she has need to go back to the school of mental discipline, in which she is yet but a novice ; and instead of taking upon herself the honorable title of wife, to set in humility and self-abasement in the lowest seat, seeking those essential endowments of mind and of heart, without which, the blessing of her heavenly Father must be expected in vain.

Above all other considerations then, as the bridal day draws near, this thought will suggest itself to the serious and enlightened mind—What am I seeking in the great change I am about to make? Am I seeking an escape from duty to enjoyment, from restraint to indulgence, from wholesome discipline to perfect ease?

Let us hope that these questions may be answered satisfactorily, and that the young woman now about to take upon herself the charge of new duties, has thoroughly weighed the responsibility these duties will bring along with them ; and that in an humble and prayerful spirit she is inquiring, in what way she may conduct herself, so that all the members of her household shall be united as a Christian family, strengthening and encouraging each other in the service of the Lord.

In so important an undertaking, it cannot be deemed presumptuous to determine, with the Divine blessing, to begin with a high standard of moral excellence. Whatever our standard is, we never rise above it ; and so great are the miscalculations usually made in a prospective view of married life, that one half at least of its trials, temptations, and hindrances to spiritual advancement are entirely overlooked. Besides which, so much of the moral and religious character of a household depends upon the female who controls its domestic regulations, that the woman who should rush heedlessly into this situation, expecting to find it easier to act conscientiously than she had ever done before, would most likely be punished for her presumption by discovering, when it was too late, that instead of religious helps on every hand, she was in reality plunged into new difficulties, and placed in the midst of hindrances to her spiritual improvement, greater and more appalling than it had ever entered into her imagination to conceive.

But still there is no need to be cast down even while suffering under the natural consequences of this fearful mistake, for He who has said *commit thy way unto the Lord,* will assuredly be near in the time of trouble, when the child of sorrow, sincerely repenting of her blindness and her folly, shall meekly and fervently implore his promised aid. She will then have learned to feel, that let her confidence in the companion of her choice be what it may; let him be to her as the father she has forsaken, the brothers she has left, and the friends whose sweet fellowship she will never more enjoy; there will still be trials in her lot, in which he cannot participate, and depths in her soul which he cannot fathom. He may take her to his bosom as the shepherd takes the lamb; but the green pastures and the refreshing dew will not be his to give. He may guard her safety as the soldier guards the camp; but her enemies may be too subtle for his eye, and too powerful for his arm. He may be to her as the morning to the opening flower; but the sun which gives that morning all its light, will be high in the heavens, and if he shines not, there will be no real brightness in her day. And all this insufficiency may still be felt without a shadow being cast upon her earthly love. Indeed, we never err more fatally, or do greater injustice to the nature and attributes both of religion and of love, than when we blend them together, and expect from one what the other only can bestow. If love sometimes assists us by rendering certain portions of the path of duty more alluring, in how many instances does it throw all its allurements on the opposite side; and in such cases, how hard it is that religion should be charged with the sad consequences which are liable to follow!

I speak not here of love as what it might be, but as what it is. I speak not of that holy and seraphic ardor, which a guardian angel might be supposed to feel for the welfare of the being whose earthly course it watched with unceasing care; nor yet of that pure sentiment, scarcely less earthly in its tendency, the chastened and subordinate attachment of a redeemed and regenerated soul; I speak of love as a fitful and capricious passion, asserting unreasonable mastery over the human mind, rejecting all control, mixing itself with all motives, assuming all forms so as to work out its own purposes, and never failing to promise an earthly paradise to its blind followers.

It is of such love, I repeat, that it must be kept apart from that great work which religion has to do alone, because the strivings of the spirit in its religious exercises can only be fully known and appreciated by Him who was in all points tempted as we are; and because these groanings, which cannot be uttered to any human ear, are mercifully listened to by Him who is touched with a feeling of our infirmities.

It is highly important, therefore, that the woman who ventures to become a wife, should not be leaning upon the frail reed of human love for her support. Indeed, it is more than probable that her husband will himself require assistance; and, excellent as he may have hitherto appeared to herself and others, it is equally probable that on a nearer inspection there will be found in his religious character defects and inconsistencies, which will present insuperable obstacles in the way of her whose dependence has been solely upon him. If, however, her dependence has been rightly placed upon a higher foundation than that of human excellence or human love, these defects of character will neither hinder nor discourage her. To work out her own salvation with fear and trembling, will be the great object of her life; and while engaged with all her energies in this first duty, she will be more occupied with anxiety to draw others along with her, than with disappointment at their being less perfect than she had imagined them.

As we must all die alone, so must we live in our spiritual experience.

" Not even the tenderest heart, and next our own,
Knows half the reasons why we smile or sigh.

Each in his hidden sphere of joy or wo
Our hermit spirits dwell, and range apart;
Our eyes see all around in gloom or glow,
Hues of their own, fresh borrowed from the heart."

Human sympathy may do much to comfort, human advice to guide, and human example to encourage; but whether married or single, whether associated with others, or separate and alone; we must all bear our own burdens, perform our own duties, answer to our own consciences, reap our own rewards, and receive our own sentence at the bar of eternal judgment.

If this be an awful, and in some respects a gloomy thought, in others it is most consoling; for we need in reality but one Friend in our religious experience. All others are liable to fail us in the hour of need, and at best they can do little for us. But with this Friend on our side, no one can hurt or hinder us. Under his protection, whatever wounds we receive from any mortal foe, our immortal nature will remain uninjured. This Friend then is all-sufficient, and, blessed be his holy name, he *ever liveth to make intercession for us.*

CHAPTER II.

THE FIRST YEAR OF MARRIED LIFE.

ONE great fault which the writer of these pages has already presumed to find with female education, as conducted in the present day, is, that it fails to prepare the character, and to form the habits, for those after duties, which are as rigorously exacted, as if the whole training of youth had been strictly in accordance with the requirements of middle life. The tone of common conversation, and the moral atmosphere of general society, are strongly tinctured with the same fault—a tendency to encourage thoughts and feelings, wholly at variance with the line of conduct pointed out by religion, and even by common sense, as that which is most likely to be conducive to ultimate happiness.

But in no other circumstance of life is this want of prospective discipline at once so obvious, and so lamentable, as in the whole progress of that system of self-recommendation which men call courtship, and which unquestionably deserves that name, if to win the partial favor of an inexperienced, and perhaps a vain woman, be the only object they have in view. It is true, that the man who wishes to gain the affections of a woman, must first endeavor to render himself agreeable to her; but all I would ask is, that while endeavoring to gain her love, he should at the same time take some pains to make her worthy of his own, by treating her at least with the faithfulness and sincerity of a friend. Nor need he fear that he shall be a loser in the end by this mode of treatment, for how much greater is the flattery of being loved in spite of our faults, than of being supposed to have none!

If men would, then, in common honesty, state what points they object to in the woman they admire, and what they really do require in a wife, they would not only find their influence, during the season of courtship, productive of the most beneficial consequences, but they would themselves escape a world of disappointment afterwards, while they would save the object of their affections all that astonishment, and wounded feeling, which naturally arise out of finding herself convicted of innumerable faults which were never so much as hinted at before.

Instead of the candid and generous treatment here recommended, how often is the progress of courtship no better than a system of fulsome adulation, and consequently of falsehood, carried on exactly as if marriage was indeed the end, instead of the beginning, of their mutual existence. And thus the affair goes on—nay, it becomes even worse, until the near approach of that day which is to make them one; for friends and relatives now take the same tone, and the bride elect is set apart from all domestic discipline, the recipient of flattering attentions, the object of universal interest, and the centre towards which all calculations and all expressions of kindness equally tend.

Persons sometimes *appear* least selfish when their self-love is fully and freely gratified ; because they have then nothing left to require or to complain of. Thus the bride elect always *appears* amiable, because everybody waits upon her, everybody flatters her, and everybody promotes the gratification of her wishes to the utmost of their power. There is now no self-denial, no giving place to others, no privation of the expected means of enjoyment—or, to sum up all in one word, there is no *neglect* to try her selfishness, or put her meekness to the test. How should she be otherwise than amiable ?

In this manner time passes on, self being made daily more and more the object of universal attention, until at last, the bride becomes personally almost an idol, so lavish is the expenditure bestowed upon her now, compared with what it has ever been before; so attractive, so becoming, is every ornament she wears ; and so lively is the interest, so profound the respect, with which she is treated on that eventful day, which dawns upon her departure from her parents' home.

Far be it from me to attempt to divest that day of its solemn and important character, or to lower the tone of feeling with which it ought to be regarded ; but as a lover of truth, and a somewhat studious observer of the days which follow, I own I should like to see the preparation of a bride consist more of mental discipline than of personal adornment—more of the resources of a well-stored understanding, already thoroughly informed on the subjects of relative position and practical duty ; and with these, the still higher ornament of a chastened spirit, already imbued with a lively consciousness of the deep responsibilities devolving upon a married woman. After such a preparation, there would be no unwelcome truth to reveal, no unexpected reproof to endure. To fall short of the high standard of excellence in almost every act, and not always to be graciously forgiven, would be a matter of calculation, which, with true Christian meekness, she would be prepared to meet; while to set aside all selfish considerations, and to look almost exclusively to the happiness of others for her own, would already have become so habitual as to require no new effort to carry out through the intercourse of daily life.

Happy, and wise as well as happy, would that man be, who should make himself content to wait for the dawning of his bridal day, until the woman of his choice should have been thus prepared. But instead of this, man eagerly secures his prize ; and, like the training of a snared bird, that discipline must all come afterwards, which is to end in domestic harmony, or domestic strife.

But let us turn the page, and after welcoming home the happy couple from the wedding tour, let us venture to whisper into the ear of the bride a few sage words, from which, whether properly prepared or not, she may possibly, from the simple fact of her inexperience, be able to gather something for her future good.

If ever, in the course of human life, indecision may be accounted a merit rather than a defect, it is so in the conduct of a young and newly married woman. While every circumstance around her is new and untried, the voice of prudence dictates caution before any important step is taken, either with regard to the formation of intimacies, or the general style and order of living. A warmhearted, dependent, and affectionate young woman, ardently attached to her husband, will be predisposed to lean upon the kindness of his relatives, and even to enter rashly into the most intimate and familiar intercourse with them. But even this amiable impulse should be checked by the remembrance, that in all such intimacies, it is much more difficult to recede than to advance, and that when familiar intimacy is once established, there is no such thing as drawing back without personal affront. It will happen, too, unless the husband's relatives are something more than human, that among themselves there will not be perfect unanimity of feeling. They will probably be divided into little parties, in which individuals on one side will look with partial or censorious eyes upon the sayings and doings of those on the other. Such partial views, when they give a tone to general conversation, are very infectious, and a sensitive mind much interested, and keenly alive to impressions from such a quarter, will be but too likely to become suddenly and powerfully biased by the same prejudices which pervade the circle into which the youthful bride is introduced.

Nothing, however, can be more injudicious than for her to take part in these family matters. If possible, she ought to wait and see for herself, before her opinion is formed upon any of the subjects in question. And this, by great care, may be done without any violation of that respectful behavior which she ought to lay down for herself as a rule, in associating with her husband's relatives, and from which she ought never to deviate, let her opinion of their merits and attractions be what it may.

It is sometimes supposed that the maintenance of personal dignity is incompatible with this exercise of respect towards others. But on no subject do young people make greater mistakes, than on that of dignity. True dignity must always be founded upon a right understanding of our own position in society; for the presumption which would assume what properly belongs to another, and what in no way appertains to the individual who makes this lamentable mistake, is as far removed from dignity, as from right feeling and common sense. As a wife, then, a woman may be always dignified, though, simply as a woman, she may at the same time be humble, and as a Christian self-abased. As a wife—as the chosen companion of an honorable and upright man, it is her duty so to regulate her whole conduct, that she shall neither offend others, nor bring offence upon herself; and this is never more effectually done, than by standing aloof from family disputes, and taking no part either in the partialities or the prejudices of those with whom she is associated.

It is perfectly consistent with personal dignity, that a wife should in all respects be the mistress of her own house. If, therefore, the husband's relations have been accustomed to take part in his domestic concerns, it is highly important that they should do so no longer. Correct-minded persons will need no hint of this kind from the wife herself. Such persons will be sufficiently aware, that the interior of her establishment must be kept sacred to her alone; and that, while the greatest freedom is maintained both in asking and in granting favors, there must be no intrusion on their part into the mysteries of the kitchen, the store-room, or the pantry, without an invitation from the mistress, either expressed or implied.

Should there be wanting in the husband's relatives this peculiar kind of delicacy of feeling, it will be necessary to devise some plan calculated not to offend, by which they may be made to understand that you do not wish them, in your own house, entirely to share all things in common; for let the degree of kindness on both sides be what it may, your education and theirs will in all probability have been so different, that circumstances must necessarily arise, calculated to draw forth remarks which cannot always be acceptable; and it is therefore your wisest plan, to draw the line of demarcation on the side of safety.

Nor is it necessary that in thus asserting your rights, suspicion should be awakened of any want of kindly feeling. To obviate all chance of this, it would be wise to take advantage of the advice of your husband's relatives in all cases where they are willing to give, and where you are prepared to adopt it; and, at the same time, to be careful that an excess of kindness should accompany that uncompromising defence of your own dignity, which every woman has a right to make. No room will then be left for complaint, and you will enjoy the satisfaction of showing your husband how highly you esteem his relatives, and how much you are prepared to serve and to oblige them for his sake.

It is a painful fact, and one of vulgar notoriety, that all eyes are fixed upon a bride, some to see how she is dressed, others to observe how she behaves, and not a few to ascertain, as far as they are able, whether she has come from a respectable home, or, in other words, whether she has raised herself in worldly circumstances by the connection she has made. This exercise of idle and impertinent curiosity might appear a little too contemptible to be met with any kind of consideration, were it not the interest of a married woman to impress her new relations with an idea of her previous importance, and her unquestionable claims to respect. Even servants are much influenced by this impression, and it was, therefore, a prudent plan adopted by our grandmothers, and still kept up in some parts of England, for the bride to go well appointed to her husband's home, well supplied with a store of good household linen, and with abundance of such clothes as are not likely to become useless by being unfashionable. These things are accustomed to be discussed among servants and dependants. From one little circle of kitchen or laundry gossip, they extend to another; and well if they do not find their way through the same channel to the parlor fireside; well, if the humiliating remark is never made there, that the bride left every thing of importance to be purchased with her husband's money.

Although it may seem rather an ungracious sort of warning, thus to prepare the young bride for a kind of critical inspection scarcely consistent with kind and generous feeling, it is nevertheless necessary in such a world as ours, to calculate upon much which the external aspect of society would scarcely lead us to expect. Yet we must not for this reason forget the many instances in which the most sincere and cordial kindness is called forth on the part of the husband's relatives, when they welcome to her new home one who is literally received into the bosom of their family, and cherished as a lamb of their own fold.

In the majority of cases, too, it happens that the bride is no stranger, that her family and her husband's have been in habits of intimacy, and that the admission of this new link is but the strengthening of that intimacy into more enduring and affectionate union on both sides. In both these cases, the bride has much to console and to support her in the duties she has undertaken; and a young heart can scarcely fail to feel impressed with gratitude for this voluntary offering of a new and lasting home, with all its kindred associations of parents, brothers, sisters, and friends.

If, on the one hand, it is not only lawful but expedient to endeavor to maintain that dignity which properly belongs to a married woman; on the other, it is necessary to act with the most scrupulous regard to that minute and delicate line, beyond which dignity degenerates into a mere assumption of importance. It is unquestionably an honorable distinction to be the chosen companion of an enlightened and good man; but we must not forget, that nature never yet formed any woman too destitute of attractions, or sent her forth into the world too meanly endowed, for her to be chosen as a wife. The dignity derived from marriage can, therefore, only be a reflected one; and has nothing whatever to do with the merits or the capabilities of the married woman.

I once heard a newly married lady complaining in company with great vehemence of something which had been said to her by a single sister, and concluding many of her sentences with this remark—"All that Miss B— said was, I dare say, sensible enough; *but I, you know, am married*"—as if that alone had been sufficient to give weight to the scale in which good sense, and almost every other good quality, appeared to be wanting.

In no part of the conduct of the bride will keen eyes be more scrutinizing than here. The husband's relatives especially will be ready to detect the least assumption of superiority to themselves. If, therefore, there has been any difference of rank or station in favor of the bride, she will act most wisely as regards herself, and most generously as regards her husband, by keeping every sign or evidence of her having filled a more exalted station entirely out of sight.

All her eccentricities, too, must share the

same fate, at least, until her new relations shall have learned to love her well enough to tolerate them for her sake. At first there will be no such charitable feeling extended towards those peculiarities of character with which they cannot sympathize, perhaps because they cannot understand them. She must now be judged of by a new rule. Singularities of manner, scarcely perceived at home, or kindly borne with as a necessary part of individuality, will now appear not only glaring, but inconsistent and absurd. Faults of temper, too long, and perhaps too leniently indulged, will now be met with opposition, and have the necessity of their existence called in question; while all those little playful sallies of local wit or humor, which were wont to fill up the blanks of social life, may possibly be heard without a smile, or wondered at as unmeaning, and in bad taste.

It is unquestionably the best policy then for a bride to be in all things the opposite of eccentric. Her character, if she have any, will develop itself in time; and nothing can be gained, though much may be lost, by exhibiting its peculiarities before they are likely to be candidly judged or rightly understood. In being unobtrusive, quiet, impartially polite to all, and willing to bend to circumstances, consists the great virtue of a bride; and though to sink, even for a short time, into an apparent nonentity, may be a little humbling to one who has occupied a distinguished place amongst her former friends, the prudent woman will be abundantly repaid, by being thus enabled to make her own observations upon the society and the circumstances around her, to see what pleasant paths she may with safety pursue, or what opportunities are likely to open for a fuller development of her powers, either natural or acquired.

With regard to the duties of charity, and indeed of kindness in general, the cordial reception a bride usually meets with, the interest she has so recently excited, and the favorable aspect worn by every thing around her, naturally inspire in her mind so much that is agreeable in return, and awaken on her part so many feelings of kindness and good-will, that she becomes more than usually anxious to manifest her benevolence, even towards persons, who, under less favorable circumstances, would have excited no interest whatever.

Those who make it their business to check such feelings, have a hard and ungrateful duty to perform; and yet, where the foundation of such acts of benevolence as are thus performed, is feeling only, the danger is, that a system of behavior will be rashly adopted, which the emotions of after life will not be sufficiently powerful consistently to maintain; and the consequences of such falling off will necessarily be, that the sorrowful or the indigent will have to endure a degree of disappointment or neglect, for which they were but little prepared.

There can be neither injustice nor unkindness in not listening, in the first instance, to claims which you are not able to satisfy; but there is cruelty—absolute cruelty, in withdrawing your attention and interest from persons who have learned to look to you for sympathy and cordial feeling, and in refusing your assistance to those who have learned to look to you for support. As each person can only satisfy a certain number of claims, it follows as a necessary consequence, that by engaging at once in too many, some, or perhaps all, must in the end be suffered to fall into neglect.

The first year of married life may justly be regarded as not likely to present one half of the claims upon individual or household charity which will follow in the second and the third; would it not, therefore, be wise to lay by against a future day, a little fund or store for this purpose? and by always keeping something in hand to be appropriated to charitable uses alone, there can be no surprise when the payment of a bill is due, to find that part of the amount has already been given to relieve a family in distress, and that the payment of the whole must therefore be deferred. All such miscalculations, and falling short of funds as these, cannot be too scrupulously guarded against; for not only is their influence bad, as they operate against the prompt discharge of pecuniary debts, but their tendency is equally to be feared, as they often warp the mind from its benevolent and kindly purposes, by a frequent repetition of regret that sums have been thoughtlessly expended in charity, which ought to have been otherwise employed.

And here I would observe, that the less we are induced by circumstances to grudge our past charities, or regret our past kindness, the better it is for our own hearts, and for the general tone and temper of our minds. Indeed, where acts of charity are performed with right motives, not for the applause of men, or even for the satisfaction of having done a good deed, or brought about a good end ; but simply from a love to God, and in obedience to his commands, there can be no such thing as looking back with regret to the act itself, whatever its consequences may be. He who has commanded us to visit the fatherless and the widow in their affliction, has not given us more than human penetration to judge of the exact amount of their necessities, or their deserts. If, therefore, we have erred, it has only been in the proportion, or the application, of our bestowments. The act of giving remains as much a duty as ever, and to her who has learned to look upon the good things of this life as only lent to her for a brief season of trial, this sacred duty will be found connected with the highest enjoyments of which, in our present state of existence, we are capable.

But in order to enjoy the luxury of giving with the greatest zest, it is highly important that we attend to the strict rules of economy. I have already written much, and would that others would write more, and better, on this subject; for until we can separate in the minds of young women their favorite idea of lavish expenditure, from that of generosity, there is little good to be expected from the Wives of England, and little happiness to be looked for in their far-famed homes. Would that philanthropists of every description then, would give their attention to this subject in detail, and lay it before the public

in a manner that would render it intelligible to the female part of the community ; while, communicated through them, it would find its way to every house and every cottage in our land—not that economy which would lead to a useless hoarding up of money, but to the glorious object of effecting the greatest possible amount of good with the smallest means.

Until this most refined and delicate art is made systematically a part of female education, we must look to that stern teacher experience, to show us, late in life, what might have been accomplished by a combination of economy with kindness, had we but begun the study of this delightful art in time. We must look to the items that have been absolutely wasted, in almost every thing we have had to do, for want of being acquainted with a better mode of doing it ; and, adding these together, we must look to the helpless and the destitute, and see what an amount of suffering might have been relieved by our economy, if through a long lifetime we had turned every thing committed to our care, or granted for our use, to the best possible account. But we must look beyond this. Yes, we must look with blushing and confusion of face to that want of moral rectitude which rendered us worse than ignorant of the mischief we were doing —to that culpable and degrading apathy—that recklessness of all responsibility with which we conducted our domestic and personal affairs, regardless of each item wasted, until the whole became a mighty and fearful mass of evidence against us, perpetually reminding us, through the medium of our penurious charities, our scanty means, and our apprehensions of the fearful reckoning of each coming day—reminding us by these humiliating remembrancers of what we have lost beyond all possibility of recovery.

I am not, however, one of those who would recommend the sacrifice either of comfort or respectability for the sake of economy. A certain air of comfort, a certain degree of respectability, regulated by the sphere in which the parties move, should never be lost sight of by the mistress of a house. More especially, there should be no meanness behind the scenes, to support an unwarrantable display in public. There is a moral degradation in such meanness wherever it exists; and those persons who have habitually to hide themselves, or to conceal their dinner-table, when a guest approaches, must be living either above or below the line which strict integrity would point out to be observed—they must either be making a figure at other times, and in other places, which they are not able consistently to support; or they must be dressing and living beneath that standard of respectability which properly belongs to their character and station.

In order to proportion all these matters fairly, the bride must be content to wait until time and experience shall have brought to light her true position, and her actual means. The first year of married life will probably be less expensive than the second, and the second less so than the third. Her household furniture, and her own clothing, being good and new, there can be little wanted for repairs; and, therefore, in her domestic expenditure, as well as in her charities, this year will afford no true criterion of the claims she must afterwards expect.

It is, perhaps, owing to this fallacious appearance in their domestic affairs, that so many inexperienced persons are led on to purchase first one article of luxury or indulgence, and then another, even after their better judgment had dictated that such things should be done without; and thus, because they did not find housekeeping at first so expensive as they had anticipated, they have launched out into extravagance which they have had bitterly to regret. Such persons are apt to say, "there can be no loss in furniture, each article will always sell for its full value—there can be no waste in silver, because it is easily got rid of for the price of its own weight." But what absurdity is this! As if, after having made a certain figure before the world, and in society, it was as easy to retreat and sink into a lower grade, as it is to sell a sofa, or a silver fork. Why, this very act of assuming a certain position, and this very dread of falling back, is what the whole world is striving about at this very hour. It is what so many heads are calculating upon, what so many hands are working out, and what so many hearts are beating for. Whether we look at the wear-and-tear of mental and animal life in our great cites, our ships upon the ocean, our laborers on the land, our congregated thousands pent up in heated rooms, and our miners digging in the bowels of the earth; or whether we turn the page of man's history, and looking at the inner movements of this great principle, behold him in his moments of unrest, note down the fluttering of his ambitious hopes, the agony of his suspense, his disappointment or his triumph, it is all the effect of one great cause, and that the strongest and most universal which prevails in highly civilized communities—a desire to keep advancing in the scale of society, and a dread of falling back from the position already held.

Let us then at least talk common sense; and in doing this, I would advise the newly married woman to look at things in general as they really are, not as they might be. She will then see, that nothing is more difficult to human nature, than to come down even one step from any height it has attained, whether imaginary or real. If, therefore, the appearance a young couple make on their first outset in life be ever so little beyond their means, so far from their being willing to reduce their appearance or style of living to a lower scale, they will ever afterwards be perplexed by devices, and harassed by endeavors, to maintain in all respects the appearance they have so imprudently assumed. This perpetual straitness and inadequacy of means to effect the end desired, is of itself sufficient to poison the fountain of domestic concord at its source. It is bad enough to have innumerable wants created in our own minds which our utmost efforts are unequal to satisfy; but it is worse, as many thousands can attest, in addition to this, for the husband and the wife to be perpetually disputing at their own fireside, about what expenses can be done without, and what cannot. Yet all these consequences follow, and worse, and more calamitous than tongue or pen can describe, from the simple fact of having begun a new establishment on too expensive a scale.

It may seem like a fanciful indulgence of morbid feeling, but I own my attention has often been arrested in the streets of London, by a spectacle which few ladies would stop to contemplate—a pawnbroker's shop. And I have imagined I could there trace the gradual fall from these high beginnings, in the new hearth-rug scarcely worn, the gaudy carpet with its roses scarcely soiled, the flowery tea-tray, and, worst of all, the bride's white veil. What a breaking-up, I have thought, must there have been of some little establishment, before the dust of a single twelvemonth had fallen on its hearth!—these articles perhaps disposed of to defray the expenses of illness, or to satisfy the very creditors of whom they were obtained on trust.

Now, though I imagine myself to be addressing a class of persons far removed from all liabilities of this kind, yet, proportioned to their higher respectability, is their greater influence; and just so far as that influence is on the side of prudence and economy, will their example operate beneficially upon the classes beneath them.

It seems to be the nature of evil universally to diffuse itself, by rendering one wrong action almost necessary to another. Thus no human being can say, "I will commit this particular sin, and go no further." Most especially is this the case with every kind of deception, just as one wilful deviation from truth draws after it a long train of falsehood. Every deviation from the line of integrity, is followed by the same inevitable consequences, and thus where persons have made up their minds to exhibit before the world a style of dress, or a mode of living, beyond what their circumstances are able consistently to support, an endless train of meanness, artifice, and practical falsehood, is almost sure to follow. How much better is it then, to begin the world with an honest heart and a clear conscience, as regards these points of duty, and neither to carry on

behind the scenes a disgraceful system of extracting from comfort what extravagance demands, nor of exhibiting at first a transient display of luxury or pomp, to be repented of for the remainder of life.

All this, however, requires some self-denial, much principle, and much love. It requires self-denial, because while almost all the world is progressing at this rate, to assume a plainer and more simple mode of living necessarily brings with it a suspicion of being unable to live differently. It requires principle, because temptations present themselves on every hand to purchase what we wish for at less than its apparent value; and it requires love, because with true and deep affection, the wife is so bound up in the interests of her husband, that all things become light in comparison with his temporal and eternal good. Love, therefore, is admirably calculated to lessen all privations arising from a conscientious adherence to strict integrity on these points.

Nothing shows more plainly the mistake under which people in general labor, with regard to the degree of mental and moral capability requisite in a really good wife, than the common expression used to describe a merely well-disposed and ignorant female, when it is said of her, that she is "a good sort of body, and will make an excellent wife." The generality of men, and even some of the most intelligent amongst them, appear peculiarly disposed to make the experiment of marrying such women, as if the very fact of their deficiency in moral discipline, and intellectual power, was of itself a recommendation rather than otherwise, in the mistress of a family; and until women shall really find themselves neglected by the loftier sex, and actually consigned to oblivion, because they are indolent, selfish, or silly, it is to be feared that books may be multiplied on this subject, and even sermons preached, with little or no effect.

Still there is surely something in the deep heart of woman capable of a nobler ambition than that of merely securing as a husband the man she most admires. To make that husband happy, to raise his character, to give dignity to his house, and to train up his children in the path of wisdom—these are the objects which a true wife will not rest satisfied without endeavoring to attain. And how is all this to be done without reflection, system, and self-government? Simply to mean well, may be the mere impulse of a child or an idiot; but to know how to *act* well, so as that each successive kind impulse shall be made to tell upon the welfare and the happiness of others, is the highest lesson which the school of moral discipline can teach.

Nor is it only by the exercise of a high order of talent that this branch of wisdom can be attained. It is by using such talent as we have, by beginning early to observe and to think, to lay down rules for self-discipline, and to act upon them, so that in after years they shall have become too familiar and habitual to require an effort to maintain. Thus it is unquestionably better that the great work of mental discipline should be commenced after marriage, than not at all; but the woman who delays this work until that time, is not much wiser than the man who should have to learn to walk after he had engaged to run a race.

Already, even in the first year of married life, all the previously formed habits a woman has indulged, begin to tell upon a larger scale than they could have done in her single state. The art of economizing time may now be made to yield a mine of wealth, beyond what riches alone could ever have bestowed; and of this most precious treasure, neither change of fortune, nor place, nor circumstance, will be able to deprive her. If that cleverness which I have attempted to describe in a previous work* has been acquired and practised in her early years, it will now have become like a part of her nature—an additional faculty, which is really nothing less than the power of turning every thing to the best account; and this power she will now be able to exercise at will, for

* The Daughters of England.

the benefit of all with whom she is associated.

"But of what use," some may be inclined to ask, "is her learning and her knowledge, now that the actual work of the hand has become a duty of such important consideration?" I answer, that the early attainment of learning and knowledge will be found of more than tenfold importance now; because, in the first place, there will be no longer time for their acquisition; and in the next, they will be wanted every day, if not in their direct, in their relative exercise, to raise the tone of social intercourse around the domestic hearth.

Music, painting, and poetry, taste, tact, and observation, may all be made conducive to the same desirable end; for if by the marriage vow, you hoped to unite yourself to an immortal mind—and I cannot believe of my countrywomen that more grovelling thoughts would be theirs at that solemn hour—you must desire to sustain and cherish such a mind, in all its highest aspirations, and in all its noblest aims. In fact, I know not what love is, if it seeks not the moral and intellectual perfection of its object—if it is not willing, in order to promote this glorious purpose—

"To watch all time, and pry into all space;"

so that no opportunity may be lost, and no means neglected, of raising the tone of a husband's character to the highest scale which man is capable of attaining. It is true, that to comfort and sustain the body is a duty which ought never to be neglected; but the woman who can rest satisfied with this, knows little of the holy and elevating principal of real love—of that love which alone can justify any one in taking upon herself the sacred responsibilities of a wife.

Influenced by this love, the woman of right feeling will perceive, though but recently married, that her position is one of relative importance; that however insignificant each separate act of her life might have been when she dwelt alone, or as an inferior member of a family, she has now become the centre of a circle of influence, which will widen and extend itself to other circles, until it mixes with the great ocean of eternity. Thus, it is not only what she says and does, but also what she leaves unsaid and undone, which will give a coloring to futurity, so far as the influence of a wife extends; for to have neglected acts of duty, or opportunities of advice and encouragement, is in reality to incur the risk of consequences as calamitous as those which follow having spoken unwisely, or acted from improper motives.

It is a serious and alarming thought, but one which ought to be ever present with the young wife, that no servant can leave her establishment without being either better or worse for her experience there; that no party can meet beneath her roof without receiving some good or evil bias from the general tone of her conversation and manners; and above all, that the rules she lays down for the regulation of her household, the principles of justice and integrity, of benevolence, temperance, order, and Christian charity, which are there acted upon, will diffuse themselves through the different members of her household, and, flowing thus through various channels, will become the foundation of peace and comfort in other families, they in their turn disseminating the same principles to the end of time.

What a sublime — what an elevating thought! May it fill the happy bosom of every English bride, and may the closing resolution of the first year of her married life be this—"Let others do as they will, *but as for me and my house, we will serve the Lord.*"

CHAPTER III.

CHARACTERISTICS OF MEN.

In approaching this part of my subject, I cannot but feel that it is one which I have neither the understanding nor the skill to treat with ample justice. All I will venture upon, therefore, is to point out a few of those peculiarities, which women who have been but little accustomed to the society of men,

might otherwise be surprised to find in a husband. If, in pursuance of this task, what I am compelled to say, should appear in any way disparaging to the dignity of men in general, my apology must be this—that it is the very peculiarities I am about to point out, which constitute the chief difficulties a married woman has to contend with, and which, therefore, claim the sympathy of such as are anxious to assist her in the right performance of her duties as a wife.

Were all men excellent, without inconsistencies, and without defects, there would be no need for words of caution or advice addressed to the weaker sex, but especially to wives, for each would have perpetually before her, a perfect model of true excellence, from which she would be ashamed to differ, and by which she would be taught at once to admire and imitate whatever is most worthy of esteem. With gratitude we ought to acknowledge our belief, that morally and spiritually there is perfect equality between men and women; yet, in the character of a noble, enlightened, and truly good man, there is a power and a sublimity, so nearly approaching what we believe to be the nature and capacity of angels, that as no feeling can exceed, so no language can describe, the degree of admiration and respect which the contemplation of such a character must excite. To be permitted to dwell within the influence of such a man, must be a privilege of the highest order; to listen to his conversation, must be a perpetual feast; but to be permitted into his heart—to share his counsels, and to be the chosen companion of his joys and sorrows!—it is difficult to say whether humility or gratitude should preponderate in the feelings of the woman thus distinguished and thus blest.

If all men were of this description, these pages might be given to the winds. We must suppose, however, for the sake of meeting every case, and especially the most difficult, that there are men occasionally found who are not, strictly speaking, noble, nor highly enlightened, nor altogether good. That such men are as much disposed as their superiors to enter into the married state, is also a fact of public notoriety, and it is to the women who venture upon uniting themselves to such men for life, that I would be understood chiefly to address myself.

In order to render the subject more clear, I will in the first place draw an imaginary line between reasonable, and unreasonable, men. A reasonable man is one who will give a candid hearing to arguments against his own preconceived opinions, and who, when he believes himself to have good cause for acting or thinking as he does, is yet willing to be shown a better cause for acting or thinking differently. The mind of a reasonable man is, therefore, open to conviction, impartial, and comprehensive; and all these qualities, from the very nature of his constitution, he possesses in a higher degree than they can be possessed by woman. An unreasonable man is one who will think and act in a particular manner, simply because he will. If he knows any better reason why he so thinks and acts, he deems it unnecessary to disclose it, because to him this is all-sufficient; and as it is one which no argument can refute, and no opposition overcome, the woman who has to accommodate her habits to his, had need commence the preparation for her married life, by a study of patience from the book of Job.

If, as I have stated, the example and influence of a truly excellent man, are such as to render the very atmosphere in which he lives one of perpetual improvement and delight; on the other hand, there is nothing more discouraging to a woman, than to find defects in the character she has associated herself with for life, having believed it to be thus excellent. Indeed, the peculiarities of the wise, and the inconsistencies of the good, among the nobler sex, have a peculiarly startling effect upon women in general, and often prove the means of retarding their improvement, by awakening the childish and petulant thought, that if such are the best, there can be little use in striving after excellence at all.

All women should, therefore, be prepared for discovering faults in men, as they are for beholding spots in the sun, or clouds in the summer sky. Nor is it consistent with the disinterested nature of women's purest, deepest affection, that they should love them less, because they cannot admire them more.

Much allowance should be made in all such calculations, for the peculiar mode of education by which men are trained for the world. From their early childhood, girls are accustomed to fill an inferior place, to give up, to fall back, and to be as nothing in comparison with their brothers; while boys, on the other hand, have to suffer all the disadvantages in after life, of having had their precocious selfishness encouraged, from the time when they first began to feel the dignity of superior power, and the triumph of occupying a superior place.

Men who have been thus educated by foolish and indulgent mothers; who have been placed at public schools, where the influence, the character, and the very name of woman was a by-word for contempt; who have been afterwards associated with sisters who were capricious, ignorant, and vain—such men are very unjustly blamed for being selfish, domineering, and tyrannical to the other sex. In fact, how should they be otherwise? It is a common thing to complain of the selfishness of men, but I have often thought, on looking candidly at their early lives, and reflecting how little cultivation of the heart is blended with what is popularly called the best education, the wonder should be that men are not more selfish still.

With all these allowances, then, we may grant them to be selfish, and pity, rather than blame them that they are so; for no happy being ever yet was found, whose hopes and wishes centred in its own bosom.

The young and inexperienced woman, who has but recently been made the subject of man's attentions, and the object of his choice, will probably be disposed to dispute this point with me, and to argue that one man at least is free from selfishness; because she sees, or rather *hears* her lover willing to give up every thing for her. But let no woman trust to such obsequiousness, for generally speaking, those who are the most extravagant in their professions, and the most servile in their adulation before marriage, are the most unreasonable and requiring afterwards. Let her settle it then in her own mind, whatever aspect her affairs may assume at present, that men in general are more apt than women, to act and think as if they were created to exist of, and by, themselves; and this self-sustained existence a wife can only share, in proportion as she is identified in every thing with her husband. Men have no idea, generally speaking, of having themselves and their affairs made subservient to an end, even though it may be a good one. They are, in fact, their own alpha and omega—beginning and end. But all this, I repeat, is the consequence of a want of that moral training which ought ever to be made the prominent part of education.

Beyond this, however, it may be said to be a necessary part of man's nature, and conducive to his support in the position he has to maintain, that he should, in a greater degree than woman, be sufficient unto himself. The nature of his occupations, and the character of his peculiar duties, require this. The contending interests of the community at large, the strife of public affairs, and the competition of business, with the paramount importance of establishing himself as the master of a family, and the head of a household, all require a degree of concentrated effort in favor of self, and a powerful repulsion against others, which woman, happily for her, is seldom or never called upon to maintain.

The same degree of difference in the education of men and women, leads, on the one hand, to a more expansive range of intellect and thought; and on the other, to the exercise of the same faculties upon what is particular and minute. Men consequently are accustomed to generalize. They look with far-stretching views to the general bearing of every question submitted to their consideration. Even when planning for the good of their fellow-creatures, it is on a large scale, and most frequently upon the principle of the greatest good to the greatest number. By following out this system, injustice is often unconsciously done to individuals, and even a species of cruelty exercised, which it should be woman's peculiar object to study to avert; but at the same time, to effect her purpose in such a way, as neither to thwart nor interfere with the greater and more important good.

We see here, as in a thousand other instances, the beautiful adaptation of the natural constitution of the two sexes, so as to effect a greater amount of good by their joint efforts, than either could effect alone. Were an island peopled only by men, the strictness of its judicial regulations, and the cold formality of its public institutions, would render it an ungenial soil for the growth of those finer feelings, and those subtler impulses of nature, which not only beautify the whole aspect of human life, but are often proved to have been blossoms of the richest fruit, and seeds of the most abundant harvest. And were a neighboring island peopled by women only, the discord of Babel, or the heated elements of a volcano, could scarcely equal the confusion, the ebullition, and the universal tumult, that would follow the partial attention given to every separate complaint, the ready credence accorded to every separate story, and the prompt and unhesitating application of means, to effect at all times the most incompatible ends.

Those who argue for the perfect equality—the oneness of women in their intellectual nature with men, appear to know little of that higher philosophy, by which both, from the very distinctness of their characters, have been made subservient to the purposes of wisdom and of goodness; and after having observed with deep thought, and profound reverence, the operation of mind on mind, the powerful and instinctive sympathies which rule our very being, and the associated influence of different natures, all working together, yet too separate and distinct to create confusion; to those who have thus regarded the perfect adjustment of the plans of an all-wise Providence, I own it does appear an ignorant and vulgar contest, to strive to establish the equality of that, which would lose not only its utility, but its perfection, by being assimilated with a different nature.

From the same constitution of mind which leads men to generalize, and to look at every thing they contemplate on an extensive scale, they are seldom good economists. Even the most penurious, the very misers of whom we read such extraordinary accounts, appear to have had a very mistaken idea of the best means of ensuring the great object of their lives. Thus, while most anxious to avoid the least unnecessary expense, some men greatly increase the waste and the outlay of money in their household arrangements, by not allowing a sufficient number of implements, utensils, or other conveniences, and means, for the purpose of facilitating domestic operations, by making each individual thing supply the place for which it is most suitable, and best calculated to secure against absolute waste.

The master of a family is quite capable of perceiving that money for domestic purposes is often in demand ; and that through some channel or other, it escapes very rapidly ; but he is altogether incompetent—and would that all men would believe it !—to judge of the necessity there is for each particular sum, or how the whole in the end must unavoidably be increased, by making every article of household use answer as many purposes as it is capable of, without regard to fitness, durability, or strength.

But if, on the one hand, our first wish for the increased happiness of the homes of England would be, that men should let these things alone ; our next, and perhaps it ought to stand first, and be still more earnest than the other, is this, that all women should be so educated, and so prepared by the right disposition of their own minds, as to afford their husbands just grounds for perfect confidence in their understanding and right principle, with regard to these important affairs. For in the first place, without understanding, no woman can economize ; and in the next,

without being supremely anxious for the fulfilment of domestic duty, no woman will. Thus, in addition to other causes of anxiety, sufficiently abounding in the present day, throughout every department of business, hundreds and thousands of men in the respectable walks of life, have to suffer from daily and almost hourly apprehension, that a system of neglect and extravagance in their own houses, is wasting away the slender profits of their labor and their care. On the score of simple kindness, then, one would suppose that a right-minded woman would wish to spare her husband these distressing thoughts ; while, on the score of domestic comfort, ease, and independence, it is impossible to calculate the vast amount to which she would herself be the gainer, by convincing her husband that she was not only able, but determined, to manage his household expenditure with the least possible waste.

With all this, however, and often in connection with the most rigid notions of economy, men are fond of personal indulgences ; nor ought they ever to be absolutely denied so reasonable a means of restoring their exhausted energy and cheerfulness, more especially, because those who are connected in any way with business, or who have to provide by their own efforts for the maintenance of their families, are generally so circumstanced through the greater portion of each day, as to be as far removed as possible from all opportunity of personal enjoyment.

It would, indeed, be a hard thing to refuse to the husband who returns home from his desk, his counter, or his fields, the best seat, or the choicest food, with any other indulgence his circumstances may afford. Here, however, in certain families, exists a great difficulty ; for some men, and I need not say they are of the *unreasonable* class, are determined to have the indulgences, and yet are unwilling to incur the expense. From their habit of disregarding things in detail, and looking upon them only as a whole ; they are utterly unconscious of the importance of every little addition in the shape of luxury to the general sum ; and thus the wife is placed in the painful dilemma, either of denying her husband the gratification of his tastes and wishes, or of bearing all the blame of conducting her household expenses on too extravagant a scale.

There are few situations in the long catalogue of female perplexities more harassing than this; for it must ever be borne in mind, that men have a tendency to dislike the immediate instrument of their suffering or privation. And this again brings us to observe another of their peculiarities, so important in its influence upon the whole of married life, that if a woman should venture to judge of man's love by her own, she would probably commit one of the most fatal mistakes by which human happiness was ever wrecked.

The love of woman appears to have been created solely to minister; that of man, to be ministered unto. It is true, his avocations lead him daily to some labor, or some effort for the maintenance of his family; and he often conscientiously believes that this labor is for his wife. But the probability is, that he would be just as attentive to his business, and as eager about making money, had he no wife at all—witness the number of single men who provide with as great care, and as plentifully, according to their wants, for the maintenance of a house without either wife or child.

As it is the natural characteristic of woman's love in its most refined, as well as its most practical development, to be perpetually doing something for the good or the happiness of the object of her affection, it is but reasonable that man's personal comfort should be studiously attended to; and in this, the complacence and satisfaction which most men evince on finding themselves placed at table before a favorite dish, situated beside a clean hearth, or accommodated with an empty sofa, is of itself a sufficient reward for any sacrifice such indulgence may have cost. In proofs of affection like these, there is something tangible which speaks home to the senses—something which man can understand without an effort; and he will sit down to eat, or compose himself to rest, with more hearty goodwill towards the wife who has been thoughtful about these things, than if she had been all day busily employed in writing a treatise on morals for his especial benefit.

Again, man's dignity, as well as his comfort, must be ministered unto. I propose to treat this subject more fully in another chapter, but in speaking of man's peculiarities it must never be forgotten that he ought not to be required to bear the least infringement upon his dignity as a man, and a husband. The woman who has the bad taste, and worse feeling, to venture upon this experiment, effectually lowers herself; for in proportion as her husband sinks, she must sink with him, and ever, as wife, be lower still. Many, however, from ignorance, and with the very best intentions, err in this way, and I am inclined to think such persons suffer more from the consequences of their folly, than others do from their wilful deviation from what is right; just as self-love is more wounded by an innocent, than by an intentional humiliation; because the latter shows us how little we are really esteemed, while the former invests us with a certain degree of importance, as being worthy of a premeditated insult.

It is unquestionably the inalienable right of all men, whether ill or well, rich or poor, wise or foolish, to be treated with deference, and made much of in their own houses. It is true that in the last mentioned case, this duty may be attended with some difficulty in the performance; but as no man becomes a fool, or loses his senses by marriage, the woman who has selected such a companion must abide by the consequences; and even he, whatever may be his degree of folly, is entitled to respect from her, because she has voluntarily placed herself in such a position that she must necessarily be his inferior.

I have said, that whether well or ill, a husband is entitled to respect; and it is perhaps when ill, more than at any other time, that men are impressed with a sense of their own importance. It is, therefore, an act of kindness, as well as of justice, and a concession easily made, to endeavor to keep up this idea, by all those little acts of delicate attention which at once do good to the body, and sustain the mind. Illness is to men a sufficient trial and humiliation of itself, as it deprives them of their free agency, cuts them off from their accustomed manly avocations, and shuts them up to a kind of imprisonment, which from their previous habits they are little calculated to bear. A sensible and kind-hearted woman, therefore, will never inflict upon the man she loves, when thus circumstanced, the additional punishment of feeling that it is possible for him to be forgotten or neglected.

But chiefly in poverty, or when laboring under depressed circumstances, it is the part of a true wife to exhibit by the most delicate, but most profound respect, how highly she is capable of valuing her husband, independently of all those adventitious circumstances, according to which he has been valued by the world. It is here that the dignity of man is most apt to give way—here that his stout heart fails him—and here then it must be woman's part to build him up. Not, as many are too apt to suppose, merely to comfort him by her endearments, but actually to raise him in his own esteem, to restore to him his estimate of his moral worth, and to convince him that it is beyond the power of circumstances to degrade an upright and an honest man.

And, alas! how much of this is needed in the present day! Could the gay and thoughtless Daughters of England know for what situations they are training—could they know how often it will become their duty to assume the character of the strong, in order to support the weak, they would surely begin betimes to think of these things; and to study the different workings of the human heart, so as to be able to manage even its master-chords, without striking them too rudely, or with a hand too little skilled.

And after all, this great dignity of man, is not much of it artificial, or at least put on like a robe of state to answer an especial end? Yes; and a pitiful and heart-rending spectacle it is, to see the weakness of man's heart disrobed of all its mantling pride—the

utter nakedness, I might almost say, for woman has ever something left to conceal her destitution. In the multitude of her resources she has also a multitude of alleviations to her distress; but man has nothing. In his humiliation he is like a blighted tree. The birds of the air no longer nestle in its boughs, the weary traveller no longer sits down to rest beneath its shade. Nothing is left to it but the clinging ivy, to cover with freshness and beauty its ruin and decay.

It is said of woman that her imagination is easily captivated, that she is won by the hero's fame, and led on by her love of glory and distinction to follow in the sunny path of the illustrious or the great. But far more fatal to the peace of woman, more influential upon her conduct, more triumphant in their mastery over her whole being, are the tears and helplessness of man, when his proud spirit sinks within him, or when he flies from his compeers in the race of glory, to bury his shame, and perhaps his guilt, in her bosom.

I will not ask how often, after this exhibition of his weakness, after regaining his post of honor, and being received again a competitor for distinction, he has forgotten the witness of his humiliation; but I believe it is only as a wife, a mother, or a sister, that woman can be this friend to man, with safety to herself, and with certainty that he will not afterwards rather avoid than seek her, from the feeling that she has beheld him shorn of his dignity, and is consequently able to remind him of the humiliating past. For the wife it might also be a dangerous experiment, even in her fondest and most unguarded moments, to make any allusion to scenes and circumstances of this description; especially to presume upon having necessarily assumed at such times the stronger and more important part. When her husband chooses to be dignified again, and is capable of maintaining that dignity, she must adapt herself to the happy change, and fall back into comparative insignificance, just as if circumstances had never given her a momentary superiority over him.

The peculiarity already alluded to as a

characteristic of men, and as leading them to attach more importance to what is immediate and tangible, than what is remote or ideal, is one which renders them particularly liable to deception, or rather to be, what is more properly called, *practised upon*, than directly deceived; so much so, that I believe any woman who could manage her own temper, *might* manage her husband, provided she possessed his affections. I say *might*, because the mode of management by such means would be utterly revolting to a generous and upright mind. Thus, by fair speech and smooth manners, accompanied with servile and flattering subserviency in little things, some artful women have contrived to win their way to the accomplishment of almost every wish; when a single rash or hasty word, especially if it implied an assumption of the right to choose, would have effectually defeated their ends.

I have listened much when men have been discussing the merits of women, and have never heard any quality so universally commended by the nobler sex, as quietness; while the opposite demerit of a tongue too loud, too ready, or too importunate in its exertions, has been as universally condemned. Thus I am inclined to think that silence in general, and smooth speech when language must be used, are ranked by most men amongst the highest excellences of the female character; while on the other hand, those wordy weapons sometimes so injudiciously made use of, are of all things what they most abhor.

If, however, an artful woman finds it easy to practise upon her husband by the immediate instrumentality of a manner suited to his taste, this mean and degrading system of working out an end, becomes more difficult in proportion to the frequency of its detection, until at last, some men are brought to suspect that all women act indirectly in every thing they do. Hence comes that frequent answer when we ask a simple question merely for the sake of information—"Why do you wish to know?" as if it were impossible for women to be deeply interested where they

had no end to serve, and as if there must of necessity be some hidden motive concealed behind that which is made apparent. This habitual retort falls hardly upon those who never have deserved it, and not unfrequently forms a serious obstacle in the way of obtaining useful knowledge; but it is greatly to be feared that such an expression, with the suspicion it implies, would never have become habitual to men, had not the general conduct of women brought this just punishment upon them.

Indeed, there is something revolting to man's very nature in having to calculate upon that kind of petty artifice which takes advantage of unwariness and credulity, for working out a purpose, even where that purpose may not in itself be wrong. And here we are brought at once to that great leading peculiarity in man's character—his nobility, or, in other words, his exemption from those innumerable littlenesses which obscure the beauty, and sully the integrity of woman's life. From all their underhand contrivances, their secret envyings, and petty spite, man is exempt; so much so, that the mere contemplation of the broad clear basis of his moral character, his open truth, his singleness of aim, and, above all, his dignified forbearance under provocation, might often put the weaker sex to shame.

I am aware that there is much in the situation of both parties to create this difference; that undisputed power to will, and to act, is often accompanied by a kind of moral majesty, which a weaker spirit never can attain, while kept in bondage, either by fear or by absolute restraint. I am aware too, that boys, from their very infancy, are accustomed to a mode of treatment as much calculated to make them determined, frank, and bold, as that of girls is to induce the opposite extremes of weakness, artifice, and timid helplessness; but even with these allowances, I am persuaded there are broad clear features in the moral dignity of man, which it is impossible to contemplate in their strength and reality, without respect and admiration.

And a sacred and ennobling trust it is for

woman to have the happiness of such a being committed to her charge—a holy privilege to be the chosen companion of his lot—to come with her helplessness and weakness to find safety under his protection, and to repose her own perturbed and troubled mind beneath the shelter of his love.

What then, if by perpetual provocation she should awake the tempest of his wrath! We will not contemplate the thought, for there is something as fearful in his indignation, as there is attractive in his kindness, and flattering in his esteem.

Nor, in return for this kindness, are we accustomed to feel gratitude enough; for take away from social life not only the civility, but the actual service done by men, in removing difficulty, protecting weakness, and assisting in distress, in what a joyless, helpless world would women find themselves, left only to the slender aid, and the tender mercies of each other!

It is too much regarded merely as a thing of course, for men to be obliging and attentive; and it is too little remembered at what cost to them we purchase their help and their indulgence. Nor is it only in solitary instances, or for especial favorites, that these efforts have to be made. It is the sacrifice of a whole lifetime for a man to be polite. There is no fireside so warm, but he must leave it on a winter's night to walk home with some female visitor, who has probably no charm for him. There is no situation so eligible, but he must resign it if required. There is no difficulty he must not encounter, no fatigue he must not endure, and no gratification he must not give up; and for whom? All would do this perhaps for one being in the world—perhaps for more; but to be willing to do it every day and every hour, even for the most repulsive, or the most selfish and requiring of their sex—there is a martyrdom of self in all this, which puts to shame the partial kindness and disinterestedness of woman.

It may be said that the popularity of politeness affords at once its incentive, and its reward. But whence then do we receive those many private acts of unrequited ser-vice, when no other eye is there but ours to witness—no other tongue to praise? and when we ourselves would probably have been the last recipients of such favor, had our companion chosen to assume the right of selecting an object better suited to his taste?

It is from considerations such as these, and I would wish to impress them upon every female mind, that I have not included the selfishness of man among his peculiarities, though some might think the case would warrant a notice of this nature. Yet such is my conviction, that man has much to bear with from the capriciousness of woman; such is my grateful estimate of his uncalculating kindness, not less to be admired because it is expected and required; such too has been my own experience of his general willingness to oblige, where there was little to attract, and still less to reward; that whatever may be said by others, it would ill become me to lift up a voice, and that a public one, against the selfishness of men.

Let us rather look again at that nobility of which I have already spoken, and while we blush to feel the stirrings of an inferior spirit prompting us to many an unworthy thought and act, let us study to assimilate our nature, in all that is truly excellent, with his, who was at first expressly formed in the image of his Maker.

———————

CHAPTER IV.

BEHAVIOR TO HUSBANDS.

LEST the reader should suppose, from the heading of this chapter, that the *management* of husbands is what is really meant, I must at once disclaim all pretension to this particular kind of skill; not because I do not think it capable of being carried out into a system, whereby every woman might become the actual ruler in her own domestic sphere, but because I consider the system itself a bad one, and utterly unworthy of being applied to any but the most extreme cases of unreasonableness on the husband's part.

With regard to the treatment of husbands, then, so great is the variety of character to be taken into account that it would be impossible to lay down any rule of universal application, except upon the broad principles of kind feeling, integrity, and common sense. Still there are hints which may be thrown out, it is to be hoped, with benefit to the inexperienced; and many of these will refer again to the peculiarity already dwelt upon in the foregoing chapter. The tendency in men which has been described as rendering them peculiarly liable to be impressed by what is evident to their senses, must ever be consulted by the wife who would adapt herself to her husband's mood and character; and although these may vary in every individual, and in the same may change with every difference of time and place, it becomes the duty of a wife, and one would suppose it must also be her pleasure, studiously to observe what those things are, which habitually strike the attention of her husband, so as to convey to him immediate impressions of pleasure or of pain; remembering ever, that all indirect evidence of our tastes and wishes having been consulted, even in our absence, is one of the most grateful offerings that can be made to every human heart.

Thus the general appearance of his home has much to do with the complacency man naturally feels on returning to it. If his taste is for neatness and order, for the absence of servants, and for perfect quiet, it would be absolute cruelty to allow such a man to find his house in confusion, and to have to call in servants to clear this thing and the other away after his return, as if he had never once been thought of, or at least thought of with kindness and consideration, until he was actually seen.

Some men particularly enjoy the cheerful welcome of a clean hearth and blazing fire, on a winter's day; and all are more or less solicitous to stir the glowing embers themselves, rather than to see them stirred by others. I knew an excellent woman who always had her fire built up in such a manner before her husband came home, as to present a tempting crust for him to break through on his arrival; and I much question whether the good lady was not more loved for this simple act, than she would have been, had her husband found his fire neglected, and herself engaged in tears and prayers for his individual welfare.

But here again we recognise no general rule, for some men unquestionably there are, who would much prefer that their coals should be forthcoming on a future day, than thus unnecessarily expended in a bonfire to welcome their return.

Again, it is of little use that you esteem and reverence your husband in the secret of your heart, if you do not by your manners, both at home and abroad, evince this proper deference and regard. At home it is but fitting that the master of the house should be considered as entitled to the choice of every personal indulgence, unless indisposition or suffering on the part of the wife render such indulgences more properly her due; but even then they ought to be received as a favor, rather than claimed as a right.

Women, in the present day, and in houses furnished as English homes generally are, may enjoy so many advantages in the way of pampering the body, from which men, and especially those engaged in business, are debarred, that they can well afford to give up some of these indulgences to those they love; and few indeed would not rather see them thus enjoyed, than appropriated exclusively to themselves.

There is, however, one great difficulty in connection with this duty, which it is to be hoped all persons are not, like the writer, unable to solve. It is in the important question of self-sacrifice, how far this virtue ought to extend in the treatment of husbands. There is certainly nothing more beautiful to read of in books; and could every act of self-sacrifice be seen and appreciated, there would be nothing more delightful to practise towards those we love. But the question is, does it tell in any high degree upon the happiness of man? Observation of the world would lead to the conclusion that it does not, for where one husband's heart has been softened with gratitude on discovering how much his wife has suffered and denied herself for his sake, ten times that number of women have been wounded to the very soul at not having their acts of self-sacrifice valued according to their cost.

The fact is, men in general do not see these things, unless told of their existence; and then at once their charm is destroyed. Is it not better, then, to be a little more sparing of such acts, than to do them, and then grudge the expenditure of feeling they require; or to do them, and then complain of the punishment they inflict? Besides which, some luckless women go on in this way, until more and more is expected of them; the husband, in his ignorance of the state of things behind the scenes, never dreaming of what is actually suffered, but rather proposing, in his innocence, that as one thing has been so comfortably given up, another should follow, until at last there bursts upon his unhappy head a perfect storm of feeling, from her who would willingly have been a martyr for his sake, would he only have observed and pitied what she was enduring for him.

On the other hand, those women who calmly and equitably maintain their rights, for rights all women have; who, acting upon the broad principle of yielding what is due from a wife to a husband, make a clear distinction betwixt that, and what would be expected by a tyrant from his slave; who make themselves cheerful and comfortable with what it is proper for them to enjoy, neither withholding what they ought to give up, nor giving up what they cannot afford to lose; such women are upon the whole to be preferred as companions, and certainly they are themselves exempt from a world of wounded feeling, under which the more romantically generous are perpetually suffering, and at the same time weeping and lamenting that they do so.

There is, however, a most delicate medium in these cases to be observed, for when once woman loses the disinterested generosity of her character, she loses her greatest charm; and when she becomes a stickler for rights, or a monopolizer of good things, presuming upon her greater requirements as being a more delicate and fragile being than man, she may indeed be said to have forfeited all that claims for her sex our interest and our admiration. But, on the other hand, though she may not be aware of it, there is a secret and deep-seated selfishness in the wounded feeling which accompanies a generous act, on finding it not valued according to its cost. Would it not then be wise to let this maxim be our rule—that none should give up more than they are prepared to resign without grudging, whether noticed and appreciated or not.

In my remarks upon the subject of self-sacrifice, I would, of course, be understood to refer only to those trifling and familiar affairs in which the personal comfort of daily life is concerned. The higher and more sacred claims of trial and calamity with which the experience of every human being is occasionally checkered, admit neither of doubt, calculation, nor delay. Here I cannot suppose it possible that a true-hearted woman would feel the least reserve, for here it is her sacred privilege to forget herself, to count no item of her loss, to weigh no difficulty, and to shrink from no pain, provided she can suffer for, or even with, the companion whose existence is bound up with hers.

Whatever doubt may be entertained on the subject of making self, and selfish gratification, subservient to a husband's tastes and enjoyments, in all the little items of domestic arrangement, there can be none with regard to what is right in mixing in society either with friends or strangers. It is here, the privilege of a married woman to be able to show, by the most delicate attentions, how much she feels her husband's superiority to herself, not by mere personal services officiously rendered, as if for the purpose of display, but by a respectful reference to his opinion, a willingly imposed silence when he speaks, and, if he be an enlightened man, by a judicious turn sometimes given to the conversation, so that his information and intelligence may be drawn forth for the benefit of others.

It is true that a considerable portion of tact is required to manage such matters as these, without appearing to *manage* them at all; for if the husband is once made to suspect that his wife is practising upon him for the purpose of showing how good a wife she is, his situation will scarcely be more agreeable than that of the man who is made a mere lackey of in company, and called hither and thither to do little personal services for his wife, as if she had mistaken him for one of her servants, or, what is more likely, had chosen this means of exhibiting her unbounded influence over him.

Both these extremes are at variance with good taste, to say nothing of right feeling; and here, as in innumerable instances besides, we see, that if the tact I have so highly recommended in a previous work, be valuable before marriage, it is infinitely more so afterwards. Indeed there is scarcely one among the various embellishments of female character, not even the highest accomplishments exhibited by the most distinguished belle, which may not, in some way or other, be rendered a still more exquisite embellishment to married life, provided only it is kept in its proper place, and made always subservient to that which is more estimable.

Thus the most fastidious taste, when employed in selecting what is agreeable to a husband's fancy, becomes ennobled to its possessor; while those accomplishments, which in the crowded drawing-room were worse than useless in their display, may sometimes be accounted as actual wealth, to her who has the good feeling to render them conducive to the amusement or the happiness of her own fireside.

On the other hand, it is painful to hear the complaint so frequently made by married men, that their wives have ceased to touch the instrument whose keys were rendered so sweetly available in the great object of charming before marriage; and, did not kindness or delicacy forbid a further disclosure of the secrets of their lot, there is doubtless a still greater number who could speak feelingly of their regret, that the air of careful neatness, the becoming dress, and the general attractiveness of look and manner, which first won their attention, had been gradually laid aside, as advancing years and increasing cares had rendered them more necessary as an additional charm to the familiar scenes of domestic life.

Yet in spite of appearances, it is scarcely possible to imagine how there should be, in any other situation, so natural and so delightful a display of personal attractions as at home, and before the one being whom of all the world we love best; especially when we reflect that his destiny being bound up with ours, if we allow him to feel weary of our company, annoyed by our absurdities, or dissatisfied with our personal appearance, he must at the same time suffer doubly from the mortifying conviction, that these things are to remain the same to him throughout the whole of his future life or ours.

What then so natural and so congenial to the best feelings of woman, as to render this long future as pleasing in its aspect as she can? and what so degrading, and so utterly at variance with the beauty of the female character, as, having once secured a legal claim to the protection of a husband, ever afterwards to neglect those personal attractions, which comparatively few women have to be charged with neglecting in their single state? Yet of what importance is it to the careless observer we meet with in general society, how we dress, or whether we look well or ill, compared with what it is to the man who has to see us, and perhaps us alone, seated opposite to him at every meal! Of what importance is it to the stranger that we play badly, or do not play at all—that we draw without taste, and have never learned to converse with sprightliness and ease? His happiness is in no way dependent upon us. He can turn away, and forget us the next moment. But the case assumes a widely different character, when we look at it as extending through each separate hour of a long lifetime; and surely if there be a natural exultation in having charmed an indifferent person, or even a whole party, for an hour, there must be a higher, and far more reasonable satisfaction, in being able to beguile a husband of his cares, to win him from society which might divert his thoughts from home, and to render that home, not only the scene of his duties, but of his favorite amusements, and his dearest joys.

To this high purpose every intellectual attainment should also be made conducive, for there is much in the life of men, and particularly where business engages their attention, to lower and degrade the mind. There is much to render it purely material in its aims and calculations; and there is much also, in man's public intercourse with his fellow-man, to render him eager and monopolizing in that which centres in himself; while at the same time he is regardless or distrustful of others. As a rational, accountable, and immortal being, he consequently needs a companion who will be supremely solicitous for the advancement of his intellectual, moral, and spiritual nature; a companion who will raise the tone of his mind from the low anxieties, and vulgar cares which necessarily occupy so large a portion of his existence, and lead his thoughts to expatiate or repose on those subjects which convey a feeling of identity with a higher state of existence beyond this present life. ;

Instead of this, how often does the wife receive home her weary husband, to render him still more weary, by an outpouring of all the gossip she has heard through the day, of the observations she has made upon her neighbor's furniture and way of living, of the personal attentions or slights she has received, with a long catalogue of complaints against her servants, and, worse than all, ten thousand reasons, strengthened by that day's experience, why she should be indulged with some favorite article of dress or luxury, upon which her heart has long been set!

It may be said in vindication of this mode of conduct, that the occupations of men of business in the present day are such, and so pressing, as to leave them little time, and perhaps less inclination, for interesting themselves in subjects of apparently less urgent and immediate importance; and that, consequently, all endeavor to give their minds a bias in favor of nobler things, would be unavailing. But in reply to this observation, I would ask one question—Have you made the experiment? Have you ever tried whether the introduction of a new idea, appropriately and agreeably clothed, might not be made quite as agreeable as the introduction of a new article of diet, even dressed with the nicest care? Have you then made the experiment *judiciously?* for here lies the secret of all the good we can reasonably expect. If, for instance, you should begin to talk about the stars, when your husband asks for his slippers, or quote poetry when he wants his dinner, the boldest enthusiast would scarcely be wild enough to anticipate any very favorable result.

The first thing to be done in the attainment of this high object, is to use what influence you have so as not to lower or degrade the habitual train of your husband's thoughts; and the next is, to watch every eligible opportunity, and to use every suitable means, of leading him to view his favorite subjects in their broadest and most expansive light; while, at the same time, it is within the region of woman's capabilities, to connect them, by some delicate mode of association, with the general bearing of a man's interests in this world upon his interests in eternity.

It is extremely difficult in writing on this subject to convey my exact meaning, or indeed to avoid the charge of wishing to recommend, instead of pleasant, easy, fireside chat, the introduction of a dull, and dry, or perhaps dogmatical discourse, than which, nothing can be more opposed, both to the tastes and the habits of the writer, as well as to her ideas of the nice art of pleasing and doing good at the same time. Indeed that mode of conversation which I have been accustomed to describe as *talking on a large scale,* is, except on very important occasions, most inimical to the natural softness and attractiveness of woman. It is not, in fact, her forte; but belongs to a region of display in which she cannot, or at least ought not, to shine. The excellence of woman as regards her conversation, consists rather of quick, and delicate, and sometimes playful turns of thought, with a lively and subtle apprehension of the bearings, tendencies, and associations of ideas; so that the whole machinery of conversation, if I may be allowed to use such an expression, may be made, by her good management, to turn off from one subject, and play upon another, as if by the direction of some magic influence, which will ever be preserved from detection by the tact of an unobtrusive and sensitive nature.

It is in this manner, and this alone, that women should evince their interest in those great political questions which arise out of the state of the times in which they live. Not that they may be able to attach themselves to a party, still less that they may *make speeches* either in public or in private; but that they may think and converse like rational beings on subjects which occupy the attention of the majority of mankind; and it is, perhaps, on these subjects that we see most strikingly the wide difference betwixt the low views so generally taken, and those which I would so earnestly recommend. If, for example, a wife would converse with her husband about a candidate for the representation of the place in which they live, she may, if she choose, discuss the merits of the color which his party wears, and wish it were some other, as being more becoming; she may tell with delight how he bowed especially to her; and she may wish from her heart that the number of votes may be in his favor, because he kissed her child, and called it the prettiest he had ever seen. It is this kind of prattle which may properly be described as *small talk*, and which it is to be feared denotes a littleness of soul. Yet this style of talk may be, and sometimes is, applied by women to all sorts of subjects, not excepting politics, philosophy, and even religion. But, on the other hand, there is an opposite style of conversation which may be used with equal scope of application, on almost all subjects, whether high or low: and it is a truth which the peculiar nature of woman's mind renders her admirably qualified to carry out through ordinary life, that so intimately connected are our thoughts and feelings, habits and pursuits, not only with those of other beings of a similar nature, but with a state of existence in which that common nature will be more fully developed, that there is scarcely a fact presented to our knowledge, which has not a connection, either immediate or remote, with some great moral truth; and scarcely a subject brought under our consideration, which may not be ennobled by conducing, in some way or other, to the improvement of our moral being.

It will readily be perceived, however, that this exercise of the powers of conversation would be utterly unattainable to a woman of ignorant or vulgar mind—that she would alike be incapable of comprehending the desirableness of the object, and the best mode of its accomplishment. And here I would again advert to an expression not unfrequently heard among young ladies, that they do not wish to be clever; by which we are left to suppose, by their neglect of their own minds, that they mean either well-informed, or capable of judging rightly. Yet without having paid considerable attention to the improvement and cultivation of their intellectual powers, how will it be possible for them to raise the general tone of thought and conversation at their own fireside?

Although I am not one of those who attach any high degree of importance to the possession of great intellectual endowments in woman, because I believe such natural gifts to have proved much more frequently her bane than her blessing, and because they are not the qualifications of female character which conduce most to her own happiness or the happiness of those around her; yet if there be any case in which a woman might be forgiven, for entertaining an honest pride in the superiority of her own talent, it would be where she regarded it only as a means of doing higher homage to her husband, and bringing greater ability to bear upon the advancement of his intellectual and moral good.

Indeed, what is the possession of talent to a woman, when considered in her own character, separately, and alone? The possession of a dangerous heritage—a jewel which cannot with propriety be worn—a mine of wealth which has no legitimate channel for the expenditure of its vast resources. But let her find this natural and lawful medium for its exercise, and we see at once in what an enviable position she is placed. We see at once the height from which she can stoop, the costliness of the sacrifices she is consequently enabled to make, and the evidences, no less valuable, which she can thus bring forward as proofs of her affection.

Nothing, however, can be more delicate and trying than the situation of such a woman, and especially when her husband is inferior to herself; but if he should be absolutely silly, it would require more skill than the writer of these pages can boast, to know what mode of treating him to recommend; for build him up as you will before company, and much may be done in this way by the exercise of delicacy and tact, a truly groveling man will sink again, and there is no help for it. The charitable conclusion is, that a woman so situated must be content to reap the consequences of her own folly, in having made so unsuitable a choice. The best friend on earth would be unable to assist her, nor could the sagest counsel rectify her mistake.

In the case of a highly-gifted woman, even where there is an equal or superior degree of talent possessed by her husband, nothing can be more injudicious, or more fatal to her happiness, than an exhibition even of the least disposition to presume upon such gifts. Let her husband be once subjected to a feeling of jealousy of her importance, which, without the strictest watchfulness, will be liable to arise, and her peace of mind and her free agency are alike destroyed for the remainder of her life; or at any rate, until she can convince him afresh, by a long continuance of the most scrupulous conduct, that the injury committed against him was purely accidental, and foreign alike to her feelings and her inclinations.

Until this desirable end is accomplished, vain will be all her efforts to render homage to her husband as a superior. He will regard all such attempts as acts of condescension, assumed for no other purpose than that of showing how gracefully she can stoop. In vain may she then endeavor to assist or direct his judgment; he will in such a case most naturally prefer to thwart her, for the purpose of proving his own independence and his power.

The same observations will apply, though in a milder degree, to cases in which there have been any great advantages of wealth or station on the side of the wife. The most unselfish and generous consideration, accompanied with the strictest care, are necessary here to avoid giving occasion of offence to that manly pride which startles at nothing so much as owing dignity to a woman, and being reminded of the obligation.

But if, on the one hand, this situation presents a narrow and critical walk with regard to action, on the other, it affords a boundless and delightful field in which feeling may expatiate; for it is scarcely possible to imagine any consciousness more happy than that of having been the means of conferring affluence or honor upon the being we most love: and if the consequences are such as lead to a trembling apprehension of being perpetually liable to give pain, they also admit of a noble exultation in being enabled by the same means to give an adequate degree of pleasure.

With this feeling, subdued by Christian meekness, and cherished only in her "heart of hearts," it might almost be forgiven to any woman secretly to exult in being favorably distinguished; for to render illustrious a beloved name, and to shed a glory around an honored brow, is at once the most natural, and the noblest ambition, of which the female mind is capable.

In order to render more clear and definite the observations which have been called forth by the subject of this chapter, it has been almost necessary to act the ungracious part of pointing out instances of failure, rather than success. This has been done, however, with the most sincere belief, that such instances, notwithstanding the frequency of their occurrence, arise, for the most part, entirely out of ignorance, or want of thought and observation, and are as frequently accompanied by an amiable and praiseworthy desire to be in all things, such a friend and companion as a reasonable husband would wish.

And after all, what is it that man seeks in the companionship of woman?—An influence like the gentle dew, and the cheering light, more felt throughout the whole of his existence, in its softening, healing, harmonizing power; than acknowledged by any single act, or recognised by any certain rule. It is in fact a being to come home to, in the happiest sense of that expression.

Poetic lays of ancient times were wont to tell, how the bold warrior returning from the fight would doff his plumed helmet, and, reposing from his toils, lay bare his weary limbs, that woman's hand might pour into their wounds the healing balm. But never wearied knight, nor warrior covered with the dust of battle-field, was more in need of woman's soothing power, than are those care-worn sons of toil, who struggle for the bread of life, in our more peaceful and enlightened days. And still, though the romance of the castle, the helmet, the waving plume, and the

"Clarion wild and high,"

may all have vanished from the scene; the charm of woman's influence lives as brightly in the picture of domestic joy, as when she placed the wreath of victory on the hero's brow. Nay, more so, for there are deeper sensibilities at work, thoughts more profound, and passions more intense, in our great theatre of intellectual and moral strife; than where the contest was for martial fame, and force of arms procured for each competitor his share of glory, or of wealth.

Amongst all the changes which have taken place in the condition of mankind, it is then not the least of woman's privileges, that her influence remains the same, except only as it is deepened and perfected as her own character approaches towards perfection. It is not the least of her privileges, that she can still be all to man which his necessities require ; that he can retire from the tumult of the world, and seek her society with a zest which nothing can impair, so long as she receives him with a true and faithful heart—true to the best and kindest impulses of which her nature is capable ; and faithful to the sacred trust committed to her care.

And that it is so, how many an English home can witness—how many a fireside welcome—how many a happy meeting after absence painfully prolonged ! Yes, there are scenes within the sacred precincts of the household hearth, which, not the less because no stranger's eye beholds them, repay, and richly too, dark days of weary conflict, and long nights of anxious care. But who shall paint them? Are they not graven on the hearts of English wives ? and those who hold the picture there, in all its beauty, vividness, and truth, would scarcely wish to draw aside the veil, which screens it from the world.

CHAPTER V.

CONFIDENCE AND TRUTH.

WITH regard to the behavior of wives towards their husbands, there is one great end to be attained, so unmeasurably beyond all others in its influence upon their happiness and their usefulness, that all which is requisite for the promotion of their true interest, might be summed up in this one recommendation—that the wife should endeavor, before every other earthly thing, and next to the salvation of her soul, to obtain and keep her husband's confidence. Without this, the marriage tie is indeed a galling chain ; and the woman who subjects herself to it, less enviable than a real slave. With this—with the perfect trust of a nobler nature reposing on her own, woman is raised to a degree of moral elevation, which, in her single state, she never could have known; and if her own disposition be generous and grateful, she will feel it a sacred obligation not to abuse this trust.

But the great and important question arises, how is this trust to be secured? With the most ardent desire to enjoy this, the chief good of married life, and the foundation upon which all its happiness must rest, there are two ways in which woman may effectually fail—intellectually, and morally. In the first, she may fail from want of knowledge; in the second, from want of principle.

In the first instance, whatever there may be in her conduct or conversation exhibiting a want of judgment, of that perception of fitness and adaptation, which is invaluable in the female character, and of a proper acquaintance with common things, is calculated to weaken the confidence of her husband in her ability, whatever her inclination may be, to make a good wife, a prudent mistress, or a judicious mother. It is in vain complaining that this sentence is a hard one, when her heart is right, and when she really does her best. It is in vain complaining that her husband does not trust her, either with the knowledge of his affairs, or the management of her own. Confidence in one being is not a matter of choice in another. It is what we ourselves must purchase by an absence of failure on those points, in which the interests of another party are dependent upon us.

If, then, a husband finds in his wife a degree of ignorance which renders her incapable of judging rightly in common things, if he finds that she has never made any proper use of her powers of observation, that she has not been in the habit of thinking to any rational purpose, of discriminating, comparing, or drawing right conclusions from what she has seen and heard, it would be hard indeed to require him to believe that she will act with prudence and propriety as the mistress of a house; and the natural consequence is, that she must be watched, sus-

pected, and in some degree treated as a child.

If, therefore, in a previous work I have earnestly recommended to the Daughters of England an early, and diligent cultivation of their mental powers, it has not been that such embellishments of character as are classed under the head of "Cleverness, Learning, and Knowledge," or "Taste, Tact, and Observation," should merely give zest to conversation, or throw an intellectual charm over the society of the drawing-room; it is that the happy individual who possesses these advantages, may, on becoming a wife, become also a companion in whom her husband can perfectly, and at all times, confide.

There are, however, cases in which the want of this confidence falls hardly, because it is the inevitable result of circumstances, over which the wife in her single state had no control. One of these is where the mind is naturally weak; and here the wife would certainly act most wisely, by placing her actions and opinions under the direction of her husband, and allowing herself to be treated accordingly.

But there are also those, who, from no fault of their own, have, before marriage, enjoyed few advantages as regards mental cultivation. In this case, much may be done in the way of making up for loss time; and where a studious desire to do so is evinced, where a respectful and judicious reference to the husband's opinion is sometimes made, and at other times a still more judicious silence observed, these proofs of good sense and right feeling, will go a long way towards obtaining the confidence desired.

But a far more serious, and it is to be feared more frequent reason for the loss of this invaluable treasure, is a moral one. And here, so many causes meet and combine in their operation, that it would require no common degree of knowledge of the human heart to be able to point them out with perspicuity and effect. The first thing I shall specify in relation to this part of the subject is, the essential importance there is, that every husband should feel himself perfectly safe with his wife. "Safe!" exclaims the worthy helpmeet, "with whom could he be safe, if not with me? Do I not watch him, care for him, and wait upon him with a solicitude that would screen him from every approach of harm?" All this may be true enough, and yet you may occasionally have taken advantage of your intimacy, for disclosing weaknesses on his part, which need not otherwise have been known; you may have marked your occasion when company was present, for throwing out hints against him, which you dared not have uttered when alone; or you may have betrayed an evident triumph before your friends, or your servants, on obtaining over him some advantage in opinion, or argument.

Although such offences as these may appear but very trifling items, when separately enumerated, yet their number and variety sometimes make up a sum of considerable magnitude and importance, as they operate upon individual feeling, and evince too clearly a want of delicacy, generosity, or real affection. They lead, in short, to the very natural feeling, on the part of the husband, that his wife is not the bosom friend he had fondly imagined her, that she knows no perfect identity of self with him, but has separate interests to which he and his affairs are liable at any time to be made subservient.

I have already said, that the dignity of man should always be studiously maintained; but there is also a delicate and respectful manner of giving way to a husband in little things, which is the surest means of obtaining concessions on his part, in those which are of greater moment, simply because, having found his wife generally yielding, considerate, and respectful to his wishes, he cannot suppose she will differ from him without some good and sufficient reason for doing so.

Upon the same principle, a wise woman will never be too requiring. She will neither demand from her husband those personal services which are degrading to a man and a gentleman, nor weary his patience by endeavoring to tease him out of every fault; for though the great end of marriage should

be mutual improvement, it is no more than fair, that the wife should allow her husband at least as many faults as he allows her. At all events, when little defects of character, and especially such as may be called constitutional, are quietly and charitably borne with, much strength is gained 'for making a stand against those which are more serious; and the husband who is kindly permitted to rest himself, if he chooses, in an awkward position, and to wear an unbecoming coat because it is a favorite, will be all the more likely, at the solicitation of his wife, to give up habits which are really more objectionable.

All individual peculiarities, which may not exactly be called faults, should be conceded to in the same manner; always remembering, that what we allow to men on the ground of their love of importance and authority, they equal, and often surpass, in what they yield to our weakness, incapacity, and occasional perverseness. There are many of these peculiarities, that, like our own, might excite a degree of ridicule, which, however, ought never to extend beyond mere playfulness, and not even so far as that, except where it is received in the same spirit.

If it were possible to whisper upon paper, I should here avail myself of a convenient *aside*, to hint that there is often a great deal of unnecessary bustle and importance when men have any thing to do. But why should we mind that—why should we not allow them the satisfaction of feeling, that as regards the little world in which they rule supremely, all space is theirs, and all time? and if we have not patience to look on, and see the order of our house overturned, our dinner waiting, our servants called away from their work, one to fetch paper, another string, and a third to wait until the mighty affair is complete; we have at least the advantage, when the same thing has to be done again, of taking the opportunity to do it ourselves.

A respectful deportment, and a complying disposition, evinced in these and similar cases, with a general willingness to accommodate all household arrangements to a husband's wishes, making every other consideration subservient to his convenience, will ensure for the wife, who consistently does this, a large portion of that confidence upon which her influence and her happiness so much depend.

But the greatest of all claims upon this confidence has yet to be considered; and would there were no occasion, in relation to this subject, so much as to whisper these words into the ear of an English wife—Never deceive! Were all men reasonable, temptations to do so would be infinitely less than they are; for difficult indeed is the lot of that woman, who would act uprightly, whose judgment and principles are good, and who is yet thwarted by a narrow-minded, weak, selfish, or low-principled man.

Let us imagine the case of such a wife, so situated that her lord is absent for the greater part of every day. Let us imagine her, too, surrounded by a family, having the interests of children, servants, and dependents to care for, and anxious to regulate the affairs of her household according to the principles of justice and integrity. She has her own conscience for her guide in all this, and if it be an enlightened one, how is she to make all her actions accord with the views of a husband, who is unenlightened, perverse, or partial, and perhaps jealous of her influence, and consequently determined to thwart her plans? Yet how is she decidedly to oppose his wishes, consistently with the respect which is due from a wife?

Surely the situation of such a woman, could it be contemplated in all its difficulties, and under all its gloomy shades, might be sufficient to deter any one whose married lot was not yet fixed, from risking her happiness with such a man.

If a woman thus situated, could by any honest means contrive to manage her husband, so that he should *not know it*, I think the wisest advocate for the supremacy of the loftier sex, would scarcely deny her such a privilege; and unquestionably there are cases in which unreasonable husbands are made

both happier and better, by being thus managed. Besides, the general order of a household, the direction of servants, and the influence of masters and mistresses over their dependents and inferiors, require that if good sense, right feeling, and sound principles, exist on one side, they should not be made subservient to ignorance, prejudice, and caprice, on the other.

I have said that all women have their rights, and it would be wise to begin early in married life to act upon the principle, which allows to every wife a little sphere of domestic arrangements, with which the husband shall not feel that he has any business to interfere, except at her request, and into which a reasonable man would not wish to obtrude his authority, simply because the operations necessary to be carried on in that department of his household, are alike foreign to his understanding and his tastes. To submit every little act of domestic management to the opinion of a husband, would be unquestionably to have one half of them at least either defeated in their object, or immediately interdicted, from no other reason than pure ignorance of their nature, cause, and effect. Thus, unless a husband can feel sufficient confidence in his wife, to allow her to rule with undisputed authority in this little sphere, her case must be a pitiable one indeed.

I have repeated the word *little*, because I believe it is from an ambitious desire to extend the limits of this sphere, that many have brought trouble upon themselves, by having their authority called in question, more than it ever would have been, had they remained satisfied with a narrower field for its exercise.

But delicacy, and strict fairness, are both required on the part of the wife, to ensure to herself this desirable allowance of free agency, for she must remember, that her husband has also his appropriate sphere of action, and a much more extensive one than hers, in which she has no right to interfere, because, as in the case already stated, she is incapable of understanding what is necessary there; and if on both sides there should be the exercise of this delicacy and fairness, in avoiding all assumption of a right which does not exist, it is impossible but that real affection should dictate the mutual development of much, if not all, which could interest the feelings of either party.

Thus, there need be no positive concealment, for that is the last thing I would recommend; but an open, honest, straightforward way of acting, as if each mind depended upon the other, less for assistance in its own sphere, than for perfect propriety of feeling, and constant adherence to principle, in the sphere to which it more properly belonged.

It is upon a right observance of distinctions such as these, that the dignity and usefulness of the marriage state in a great degree depend—from remembering that principle must ever be the foundation of action; but that the open disclosure of every act and purpose, must ever be a matter of choice; and if regarded as such, there will be no doubt but mutual love will supply information enough to satisfy the most unbounded curiosity. Thus it has never appeared to me, that the free agency which a judicious wife should be permitted to enjoy in her own department, had any thing to do with concealment; any more than that the transactions in one public office should be said to be concealed from another, because each had its separate rooms and officers. So far from this, I should rather say that a generous nature, and especially that of woman, when implicitly trusted to, and made to feel that trust, will, from a sense of grateful satisfaction, involuntarily disclose its every plan, purpose, and act, not even throwing a veil over its many failures and short-comings in the way of discretion or duty.

Indeed, so powerful in its influence upon the female character, is this feeling of being trusted, that I have often thought if man could know the heart of woman better, he might almost guide it to his pleasure, by simply using this master-key to her gratitude and generosity. But I must not forget, that my business is with the behavior of wives to their husbands, not with that far easier subject in a female hand, the behavior of husbands to their wives.

Among other points of consideration, comprehended under the general head of confidence towards wives, there is one of such paramount importance to the rectitude of woman's conduct in her domestic affairs, that were this one consideration all which had to be taken into account, it would of itself be well worth every endeavor to ensure so desirable an end. I mean the open communication of the state of the husband's pecuniary circumstances to his wife; for I can scarcely imagine any thing more congenial to the best feelings of a faithful wife, than to be made the partaker of all the interest and enjoyment her husband derives from prosperity and success; while, on the other hand, there is no greater cruelty, than that of allowing a woman of good principles and right feelings, to go on ignorantly conducting her household expenses, in a manner inconsistent with the real state of his affairs, when they are in any degree depressed or involved in difficulty.

Yet how often has this been the case! How often has an honest-hearted woman had to bear the charge of having been in reality dishonest to her husband's creditors, when ignorance, not want of principle, was the cause! Besides which, how much may be done by domestic economy, and by a consistently meek and unpretending deportment, if not exactly to avert the calamity of a ruined house, at least to alleviate the wounded and bitter feelings which naturally arise among those who are the greatest sufferers.

The present day is one which claims peculiar attention to this subject; and if from any fault in the wife, from any betrayal of her husband's secrets, any artifice or trickery practised against himself, any assumption of unbecoming importance on her part, any want of consideration for his feelings, or foolish and presumptuous interference with matters peculiarly his own—if from any of these causes, she has shut herself out from his confidence, now, before it shall be too late, is the time to begin a new system of behavior, for which she may eventually be rewarded by being admitted into his bosom-counsels, and thus allowed to share, not only in all the hopes and fears arising out of the fluctuating nature of pecuniary affairs; but also in those nobler acts of self-denial, which accompany sound and enlightened views of the requirements of justice, in all transactions of a pecuniary character.

What, then, of such importance as to obtain the perfect and confiding trust of the companion with whom, or for whom, you have to act in every thing you do? and in order to this happy attainment, nothing is so essential as that you should yourself be true.

There is a spirit of truth and a spirit of falsehood, pervading many of those actions, which could not be said to be either true or false in themselves. Yet, according to the choice we make betwixt these, our behavior will be upright, candid, generous, and free; or it will be servile, artful, selfish, and cowardly. It does not follow, in order to practise falsehood, that we must deviate from the exact letter of truth. There are methods of deceiving, as many, and as various, as the circumstances which checker our experience every day; and if a conscientious adherence to truth is not made the rule of daily life, one act of duplicity will grow out of another, until the whole conduct becomes a tissue of artifice and deceit.

The first and most innocent step towards falsehood is concealment. Before our common acquaintances, there is wisdom in practising concealment to a certain extent; but where the intimacy is so great, the identity so close, as between a husband and a wife, concealment becomes a sort of breach of faith; and with parties thus situated, the very act of concealment can only be kept up by a series of artful endeavors to ward off suspicion or observation of the thing concealed.

Now, when a husband discovers, as in all probability he will, unless these endeavors are carried out to a very great extent—when he discovers that his wife has been concealing one thing from him, he very naturally supposes that she has concealed many more; and his suspicions will be awakened in proportion. It will then be in vain to assure him that your motive was good, that what you did was only to spare him pain, or afford him pleasure; he will feel that the very act is one which has set him apart in his own house as a stranger, rather than a guardian there—an enemy, rather than a friend.

Why then should you begin with concealment? The answer, it is to be feared, is but too familiar—"My husband is so unreasonable." And here then we see again the great advantage of choosing as a companion for life, a reasonable man, who may with safety and satisfaction be made acquainted with every thing you think or do.

After concealment has been habitually practised, there follows, in order to escape detection, a system of false pretences, assumed appearances, and secret schemes, as much at variance with the spirit of truth, as the most direct falsehood, and unquestionably as debasing to the mind.

But, as an almost inevitable consequence, next follows falsehood itself; for what woman would like her husband to know that she had, for days, months, or years, been practising upon his credulity. If he discovers what she has been concealing, he will also discover, that often when the subject was alluded to, she artfully evaded his questions by introducing another; that sometimes she so managed her voice as to convey one idea, while she expressed another; and that at other times she absolutely *looked* a lie. No, she cannot bear that he should look back and see all this, lest he should despise her; and, therefore, in some critical moment, when brought into that trying situation in which she must either confess all, or deny all, she pronounces at last that fatal word, which effectually breaks asunder the spiritual bond of married love.

And now, it is scarcely possible to imagine a more melancholy situation than that of a weak and helpless woman, separated by falsehood from all true fellowship, either human or divine; for there is no fellowship in falsehood. The very soul of disunion might justly be said to be embodied in a lie. It is in fact the sudden breaking asunder of that great chain which connects together all spiritual influences; and she who is guilty of falsehood, must necessarily be alone;—alone, for she has no sympathy of feeling with the beautiful creation around her, of which it has truly been said, that "Nature never deceives;"—alone, for in that higher world, where all her secret thoughts and acts are registered, its very light is truth;—alone, for she has voluntarily become a stranger, a suspected thing, an enemy, to that one friend in whose bosom she might have found shelter and repose.

It is a fact which scarcely needs to be repeated, that the closer the intimacy, and the more important the trust, the greater is the individual injury, and consequently the violation of personal feeling, when that trust is abused. Thus when the child is first made to understand that it has been deceived by its mother, the very life of its little soul seems for a moment to be quenched. When the father finds that his prodigal son has but returned to take advantage of his affection and credulity, his wounded spirit sinks, and his weary heart is broken. But when the husband looks with earnest eyes into the countenance whose beauty was once his sunshine; when memory flies back, and brings again her plighted vow, with all its treasury of truth; when he thinks of that fond heart which seemed to cling to his in all the guileless innocence of unsophisticated youth—oh, it is horrible "to be discarded thence," by the dark demon of distrust, perpetually reminding him, that the bright and sunny tide of early love, upon which he trusted all the riches of his soul, is but a smiling and deceitful ocean, whose glassy surface at once reflects the hues of heaven, and conceals the depths of hell.

It is impossible to speak in language adequate to the importance of this cause, for by failure in this one point, the whole fabric of connubial affection, which might otherwise be made so influential in the promotion of every kind of good, becomes a heap of ruins, as disgraceful to the deceiver as unsightly to the deceived.

Yet, after all, is not the former the greater sufferer of the two? Is it not more miserable to be thus separated from all community of thought and feeling, either earthly or divine, than to be the mere dupe of treachery or guile? Yes, and she feels it so, and out of her very desolation, sometimes awakes the voice of penitence, making confession of some individual act of transgression, and craving, with all the humility of utter wretchedness, to be reinstated in confidence and esteem. But this cannot be. The thing is impossible. The silver cord which has been loosed, no single act of human will can tie again. The golden bowl which has been broken, no single effort of human kindness can restore.

But may not years bring back the confidence so, wantonly abused? Oh, blessed thought! Begin, then, a new life. Let truth be the principle of every thought, the echo of every word, the foundation of every act. Truth is invincible—it must—it will prevail. Beautiful as the morning it will arise; glorious as the noonday it will shine forth; calm as the evening it will be followed by repose; and thus each day may feel its gladdening and invigorating influence; while every flower that grows beneath its ray will shed a charm upon the path of life.

But if the regaining of confidence after it has been lost, be an object of such immeasurable importance to attain, what must be the happiness of her who has never lost this treasure? who has borne through all change, and all trial, a true and upright heart towards her husband, who, though he may have sometimes mistaken, and sometimes blamed her, has still been able to say, even when appearances were least favorable, and when perhaps he was most in need of the consolation derived from reposing implicit confidence in her sincerity—

"Thou art my true and honorable wife,
As dear to me as are the ruddy drops
That visit this sad heart."

What, then, if she has sometimes suffered when it has seemed as if a little artifice would have made all things easy, that suffering has been in a noble cause. And then the reward! —the conscience void of offence towards that one being to whom she can be nothing, if not true—the fearless look—the unfaltering tone —the steady hand—the soul that might be mirrored forth before him—the hopes, the fears, that might be his—the workings of a busy mind, whose minutest plans might all at any moment be laid bare before his scrutinizing eye—and onward, into the far future, not a dream but he might know it all—and onward yet—the blessed consciousness that, should the secrets of all hearts be read on the great day of everlasting doom, there would be one whose glance, and that the most familiar, would not detect a single act or thought of her whole life inimical to his interests, or such as might not have been revealed to him before.

Nor is the mere escape from the uncertainty, anxiety, and pain, entailed upon the habitual practice of falsehood, all that has to be considered. A brighter picture in the page of truth, is that in which we see portrayed in living hues, the enjoyment of unburdening a full heart, and laying open its secret treasury of thought and feeling to him whose earthly portion, whether it be one of weal or wo, must inevitably be blended with our own. And it is from this very identity that the practice and the love of truth becomes more important, as a moral obligation in the married state, than in all others. Indeed the perfect truth towards each other of individuals thus united, is as necessary to their welfare and their happiness, as the union and concurrence of the different members of the human frame, is to the usefulness and integrity of the whole.

It is, as has already been stated, the peculiar privilege of a strict adherence to truth, that it brings its own reward ; for if we voluntarily confess the truth, by this means we obtain confidence ; if we suffer for truth, we have the consolation of suffering in a noble cause, and of gaining strength by every effort we make in its support; while, if we endeavor conscientiously to uphold the truth, and thus consistently exemplify the beauty

and the power of this great attribute in the Divine government, we have the still higher satisfaction of doing our humble part to glorify the God of truth.

CHAPTER VI.

THE LOVE OF MARRIED LIFE.

IF, in the foregoing pages, I have spoken of the married state as one of the trial of principle, rather than of the fruition of hope ; and if, upon the whole, my observations should appear to have assumed a discouraging, rather than a cheering character, it has arisen, in the first place, from my not having reached, until now, that part of the subject in which the advantages of this connection are fully developed ; and if, in the second place, I must plead gulity to the charge of desiring to throw some hindrances in the way of youthful aspiration, it has simply been from observing amongst young people generally, how much greater is the tendency to make the experiment for themselves, than to prepare themselves for the experiment.

If, therefore, I have selected words of warning, in preference to those of an opposite nature, it has been because the tide of popular feeling, especially amongst young women, is already sufficiently strong in favor of matrimonial alliances ; while the disposition to ensure all the advantages of such an alliance, appears far beyond what bears any proportion to the desire evinced for submitting to that discipline, by which alone they can be rendered permanent.

That this disproportion betwixt expectation and reality, arises from ignorance, rather than any other cause, I am fully prepared to believe —ignorance of the human heart, of the actual circumstances of human life, of the operation of cause and effect in human affairs, and of the relative duty of human beings one towards another.

The numbers who have failed in this way to realize in their experience of married life, the fair picture which imagination painted before it was tried, it would be useless to attempt to enumerate; as well as to tell how many have thrown the blame of their disappointment upon situation or circumstances—upon husband, servants, friends, or relatives—when the whole has rested with themselves, and has arisen solely out of a want of adaptation in their views and habits to the actual requirements of the new state of existence upon which they have entered.

That this state itself is not capable of the greatest amount of happiness which is expected from it, I should be sorry to deny; and and all I would attempt to prove in the way of discouragement is, that its happiness will often prove to be of a different kind from what has been anticipated. All that has been expected to be enjoyed from the indulgence of selfishness, must then of necessity be left out of our calculations, with all that ministers to the pride of superiority, all that gratifies the love of power, all that converts the woman into the heroine, as well as all that renders her an object of general interest and attraction.

It may very naturally be asked, what then remains? I answer, the love of married life; and in this answer is embodied the richest treasure which this earth affords. All other kinds of love hold by a very slender tenure the object of supreme regard; but here the actual tie is severed only by the stroke of death, while mutual interest, instead of weakening, renders it more secure. The love of a parent for a child, natural, and pure, and holy as it is, can never bind that child beyond a certain period within its influence; while the love of a child for a parent must necessarily be interrupted in the course of nature, by the dissolution of its earthly hold. The love of a brother or a sister must ever be ready to give place to dearer claims; and that of a friend, though "very precious" while it lasts, has no real security for its continuance. And yet all these, according to the laws which regulate our being, in their own place and measure, supply the natural craving of the human heart for something beyond itself, which it may call its own, and in the certainty of possessing which, it may implicitly repose.

Nor is that sage philosophy, which would deny the existence of this craving, or make light of its requirements. There is no moody misanthrope, however solitary the lot he chooses for himself, but cherishes within the secret of his soul, some yearning thought of how he might have been, and could have, loved. There is no agitator of public movements, hardened and sharpened by the fierce contact of contending interests, but seeks some chosen spot of rest, where the cold armor of his selfishness may be thrown off, before that being whose hand has been accustomed to pour into his breast the balm of sympathy and love. There is no outcast from the holier walks of life, no victim of its cruel vices, no maligner of religion and its sacred institutions, but acknowledges, at times, a secret impulse to cling to something more kind, more gentle, and less degraded than himself.

Nor is it only in our human sympathies that this craving is developed. The tame bird, or the pet lamb, is folded to the solitary bosom of the neglected child, with as intense a feeling, as if it knew the thoughts of tenderness pent up and aching there. The miser, whose grovelling soul is alike at enmity with God and man, enters his narrow cell, and, calling to his side his faithful dog, smiles on the unconscious animal with a look which at once reveals the history of his wasted heart. And strange to say, it is sometimes even thus with ambition, and with many of those aims and occupations which absorb man's life. They are followed, not for the results they bring, so much as for the promises they offer—for the vague hopes they hold out, that their entire accomplishment will satisfy the cravings of an insatiable soul.

But, perhaps, more than in any other case, is it thus with literary fame, in the pursuit of which how many are urged on by a strong, though it may seem to some a fanciful impression, that the voice of feeling which has failed to find an echo in its own immediate sphere, may, in the wide world through which it is sent forth, touch in some unknown breast a sympathetic chord, and thus awaken a responsive emotion.

But if with man, the most powerful and independent of created beings, there ever exists this want of spiritual reliance and communion, what must it be to the weaker heart of woman, to find one earthly hold after another giving way, and to look around upon the great wilderness of life, in which she stands unconnected, and consequently alone? If there be one principle in woman's nature stronger than all others, it is that which prompts her to seek sympathy and protection from some being whom she may love, and by whom she may be loved in return. The influence of fashion is, perhaps, of all others to which the female sex is exposed, the most hardening to the heart—the most chilling to its warm and genuine emotions. Yet I much question whether the successful candidate for public admiration, would not sometimes willingly retire from the splendid circle in which she is the centre of attraction, to receive in private the real homage of one unsophisticated, noble, and undivided heart. Having failed in this, woman's first and most excusable ambition, how often does she go forth into the world, to waste upon the cold and polished surface of society, those capabilities of thought and feeling which might, if more wisely directed, have made a happy home; and how often is she compelled to look, appalled and horror-struck, upon the utter emptiness of the reward which follows this expenditure, when the same outlay in a different soil, and under happier culture, might have enabled her to gather into her bosom a hundred fold the richer fruits of confidence and affection!

It is only in the married state that the boundless capabilities of woman's love can be fully known or appreciated. There may, in other situations, be occasional instances of heroic self-sacrifice, and devotion to an earthly object; but it is only here that the lapse of time, and the familiar occasions of every day, can afford opportunities of exhibiting the same spirit, operating through all those minor channels, which flow like fertilizing rills through the bosom of every family, where the influence of woman is alike happy in its exercise, and enlightened in its character.

Out of all which our first parents sacrificed when they lost their high estate, it was mercifully permitted them to retain their mutual love; and it is possible to imagine that the mother of mankind, even when looking her last upon that Eden whose flowers her care had tended, would turn to the companion of her banishment with a deeper and more fervent appeal to his sympathy and affection, than she ever could have felt the need of, in those bowers of beauty where a leaf was never seen to fade. Thus out of her very weakness, and from among the many snares which have beset the path of woman since that day of awful doom, has arisen a more intense desire, and a more urgent need, for the support of a stronger nature, with which her own can mingle, until it almost loses the bitter consciousness of having forfeited all claim to be still an inhabitant of Paradise.

Lest, however, the temptations to this forgetfulness should stand between her and the necessity there is to seek a higher and a holier rest, there has fallen on her earthly lot some shadows, which the light of earthly love is not sufficient to dispel. Even love itself has sometimes failed; and, worse than all, in her own bosom has become extinguished.

In order to know how to avert this calamity, it is necessary to endeavor to look calmly and dispassionately at the subject in every point of view, to dispel the visions of imagination, and to ask what is the real cause of failure, where woman has so much at stake.

Love may arise spontaneously, but it does not continue to exist without some care and culture. In a mind whose ideas are all floating at large, and whose emotions of feeling or affection are left to the prompting of impulse, unrestrained by the discipline or reason, there will naturally arise strange wandering thoughts, which will be likely at any unguarded moment to undermine so frail a fabric, as love under such circumstances must ever be.

One tendency in the mind of the married woman who has thus neglected the government of her own feelings, will be, on every occasion of momentary vexation or dissatisfaction, to compare her husband with other men to his disadvantage ; than which nothing can be more dangerous, or more inconsistent with that faithfulness which ought ever to be a leading characteristic in the love of married life. Nor can any thing well be more impolitic or absurd ; since there is no human being, however excellent, who may not, in some way or other, be made to suffer by comparison with others. Besides which, what right have we, as frail and erring creatures, to aspire, in this connection, to an alliance with a being entirely faultless, or even more perfect than ourselves ?

If then there should occasionally arise feelings of disappointment and dissatisfaction, as the lapse of time and a nearer acquaintance develop a husband's faults, it is good to bear in mind that the same exposure of your own, from the same cause, must necessarily have taken place ; and by often dwelling upon this view of the subject, a degree of charitable feeling will be excited, more calculated to humble and chasten the heart, than to embitter it against the failings of another.

Still there are frequent provocations of temper, which some men through ignorance, and others from perverseness, or the love of power, are not over scrupulous to avoid ; and these, to an irritable temperament, are often more trying than greater deviations from what is strictly right.

Against the petulance and occasional resentment which an accumulation of these trials call forth, there is one great and solemn consideration, by which a woman of right feeling may, at any time, add sufficient weight to the balance in her husband's favor —she may think of his death, of the emotions with which she would receive his last farewell, and of what would be her situation if deprived at once of his love, his advice, and

his protection. We are all perhaps too little accustomed to such thoughts as these, except where illness or accident places them immediately before us. We are too much in the habit of looking upon the thread of life with us, as far more likely to be broken first, and of thinking that the stronger frame must necessarily endure the longest. But one realizing thought that the sentence of widowed loneliness may possibly be ours—how does it sweep away, as by a single breath, the mist of little imperfections which had gathered around a beloved form, and reveal to us at one glance the manly beauties of a noble, or a generous character!

Even beauties less than these—the kind look, the cordial welcome, the patient answer, the mild forbearance, the gentle and familiar acts of every day which never-tiring affection prompted, and the smile which beamed upon us perhaps when we deserved it least—all these come back, and live before us, as often as we think of the possibility of losing them forever. And it is good to have the heart thus softened and subdued—thus made to feel how completely the petty provocations of each day would vanish from our minds, if we stood by the dying couch of him who never offended but in little things, and heard the parting benediction of the friend who would fain leave behind him a blessing, which his living presence had failed to bestow.

It is an unspeakable privilege enjoyed by the women of England, that in the middle ranks of life, a married woman, however youthful or attractive, if her own manners are unexceptionable, is seldom, or never, exposed to the attentions of men, so as to lead her affections out of their proper channel.

How much is gained in domestic and social happiness by this exemption from customs which prevail on the continent, it is here unnecessary to attempt to describe ; for I cannot imagine there is any right-minded woman, still less any Christian wife, who does not number it among the peculiar blessings of her country, and her sex. Yet even in our privileged land, where the established rules of society are so much more favorable than in others, to the purity of social morals, and the sanctity of home-enjoyments, there may occasionally occur an attempted deviation from these rules, on the part of ignorant or unprincipled men. In all such cases, however, the slightest approach to undue familiarity is easily repelled, by such a look and manner, as all women know how to make use of in discountenancing what is not acceptable; and even in more trifling cases, or where the temptation to be agreeable overcomes the inclination to be otherwise, I believe that a frank and easy manner of speaking of a husband with respect and evident affection, would answer every purpose of putting a stop to such advances; while, on the other hand, nothing can be more likely to invite them, than speaking in complaining terms either of a husband, or of his behavior towards yourself.

But the surest safeguard both at home and abroad, and the truest test by which to prove the propriety of every look, and act, and word, when mixing in the society of other men, is a sincere and faithful love for the companion of your choice. Without this, it would be vain to lay down rules by which a wandering fancy might be kept in check. An enlightened conscience alone, in such a case, can point out exactly how to act; while with this love, there needs no other guide. It is itself so pure, so constant, and so true, that conscience only echoes what its happier voice approves.

And now, having thus loved your husband, and cast in your lot with his—having chosen his portion, his people, and his God for yours, it is meet that you should love him to the last. It is true, there are cases where a gradual deterioration of character, or a sudden fall from moral rectitude, renders affection the last offering a stranger would think it possible to make at such a shrine; but if others turn away repelled, there is the more need for such a man, that his wife should love him still—there is the more need that one friend should remain to be near him in his moments of penitence, if such should ever come; or to watch the lingering light of

better days, so as if possible to kindle it once more into a cheerful and invigorating flame.

Of all the states of suffering which have ever swelled the ocean of human tears, there is none in the smallest degree comparable to the situation of such a wife; yet, as if by some law of nature, which raises the sweetest flowers from out the least apparently congenial soil, it is here that we so often see the character of woman developed in all its loveliest and noblest attributes. It is here that we see to what an almost superhuman height that character can rise, when stripped of its vanity, and divested of its selfishness. Alas! that she should wait for the chastening of a cruel scourge, before she will even aspire to that perfection of moral beauty of which her nature is capable!

If to love the vicious, or the degraded, were necessarily to love their vices too, it would be a melancholy picture to see an amiable woman falling into such a snare. But though unquestionably too many do this, and sometimes almost unconsciously assimilate themselves with vice, either from constant association with what is evil, or from the habit of referring their own judgment of right and wrong to that of a polluted and degraded mind; there are others who, with the nicest discrimination, and with the clearest convictions on these points, go on from day to day beholding what they hate, in the most intimate connection with what they love.

While contemplating the fate of such, our only consolation is to compare their situation as it is, with what it would be, were there no channel open to mercy and to hope, for the outpourings of a heavily laden heart through the medium of prayer. Friends bring no comfort, earth holds no consolation for those who weep such tears; yet often in the depth of their affliction have they been enabled to own and bless the chastening of a Father's hand, and to feel that in that very chastening there was love!

But it is time to turn our attention to that portion of the love of married life, which belongs more especially to the other sex; and here the first thing to be observed is, that no man's heart can be said to be really gained before his marriage. He may be the most obsequious of beaux, the most flattering of admirers, and even the most devoted of lovers; but his affection has not been tried in the way which brings it to the severest test. It is true it may have been tried by absence, by caprice, by coldness, or neglect; but it has yet to be tried by the security of entire possession; by the monotony of sameness; and, I grieve to add, too often by the neglect of those personal attractions by which it was at first so studiously invited.

How little do women think of this, when, by the security of the marriage tie, they are rendered careless of the preservation of the richest jewel in their bridal wreath, and one which never yet was secured to its possessor by any outward bond! How little do they reflect, that while it is the natural tendency of woman's heart to become more tenderly attached to the being with whom she is thus associated, it is not so with that of man! And thus it becomes the study of a life, to retain in all its freshness and its beauty, the precious gem committed to their trust.

Nor should we murmur that it is so. For once possessed of this inestimable treasure, and secure of its continuance, what should we aspire to beyond our present state? Even as things are, we see a marked neglect in the behavior of some wives; as if their husbands were equally bound to love, as to protect them. What then would be the degree of carelessness prevailing among women, if this were really the case, and if the heart of man invariably, and of necessity, went along with his duty as a husband!

Happily for our sex, however, there are means of securing this treasure, more efficacious than the marriage vow; and among these, I shall mention first, the desirableness of not being too requiring. It must ever be borne in mind, that man's love, even in its happiest exercise, is not like woman's; for while she employs herself through every hour, in fondly weaving one beloved image into all her thoughts; he gives to her comparatively few of his, and of these perhaps

neither the loftiest nor the best. His highest hopes and brightest energies, must ever be expected to expend themselves upon the promotion of some favorite scheme, or the advancement of some public measure; and if with untiring satisfaction he turns to her after the efforts of the day have been completed; and weary, and perhaps dispirited, comes back to pour into her faithful bosom the history of those trials which the world can never know, and would not pity if it could; if she can thus supply to the extent of his utmost wishes, the sympathy and the advice, the confidence and the repose, of which he is in need, she will have little cause to think herself neglected.

It is a wise beginning, then, for every married woman to make up her mind to be forgotten through the greater part of every day; to make up her mind to many rivals too in her husband's attentions, though not in his love; and among these, I would mention one, whose claims it is folly to dispute; since no remonstrances or representations on her part will ever be able to render less attractive the charms of this competitor. I mean the newspaper, of whose absorbing interest some wives are weak enough to evince a sort of childish jealousy, when they ought rather to congratulate themselves that their most formidable rival is one of paper.

The same observations apply perhaps in a more serious manner to those occupations which lead men into public life. If the object be to do good, either by correcting abuses, or forwarding benevolent designs, and not merely to make himself the head of a party, a judicious and right-principled woman will be too happy for her husband to be instrumental in a noble cause, to put in competition with his public efforts, any loss she may sustain in personal attention or domestic comfort.

A system of persecution perseveringly carried on against such manly propensities as reading the newspaper, or even against the household derangements necessarily accompanying attention to public business, has the worst possible effect upon a husband's temper, and general state of feeling. So much so, that I am inclined to think a greater amount of real love has been actually teased away, than ever was destroyed by more direct, or more powerfully operating means.

The same system of teasing is sometimes most unwisely kept up, for the purpose of calling forth a succession of those little personal attentions, which, if not gratuitously rendered, are utterly destitute of value, and ought never to be required.

To all married women, it must be gratifying to receive from a husband just so much attention as indicates a consciousness of her presence; but with this acknowledgment, expressed in any manner which may be most congenial to her husband's tastes and habits, a woman of true delicacy would surely be satisfied without wishing to stipulate for more. Still less would she annoy him with an exhibition of her own fondness, under the idea of its being necessarily returned in kind. It is a holy, and a blessed mystery, from the secrets of which, in its mastery over the human mind, almost all women who have ever been beloved, have learned the power of their own tenderness; but in proportion to the purity of its nature, and the sacredness of its exercise, is its capability of being abused and degraded. Thus, all exhibition of fondness before a third party, may justly be looked upon as indicating a total ignorance of the intensity, and the purity, of that which alone deserves the name of love; while, could one imagine the possibility of such a thing, all exercise of this fondness made use of for the purpose of obtaining advantage over a husband's judgment or inclination, could only be supposed to arise out of the meanest impulse of a low, an artful, and a degraded mind.

But we cannot for a moment imagine such things really are. We cannot believe that a woman conscious of her personal attractions, could hang about her husband's neck, or weep, or act the impassioned heroine, for the base purpose of inducing him to make some concession, which in his calmer moments he could not be prevailed upon to grant. No, the true heart of woman knows too well, that that sweet gift of heaven, granted in consideration to her weakness, was never meant to be made use of as an instrument of power to gain a selfish end; but was permitted her for the high and holy purpose of softening the harder and more obdurate nature of man, so as to render it capable of impressions upon which the seal of eternity might be set.

It requires much tact, as well as delicacy, to know how to render expressions of endearment at all times appropriate, and consequently acceptable; and as love is far too excellent a thing to be wasted, and tenderness too precious to be thrown away, a sensible woman will most scrupulously consult her husband's mood and temper in this respect, as well as remember always the consideration due to her own personal attractions; for, without some considerable portion of these advantages, it will be always safest not to advance very far, unless there should be clear and direct encouragement to do so. Pitiful pictures have been drawn in works of fiction of the hopelessness of efforts of this nature; but one would willingly believe them to be confined to fiction only, for there is happily, in most enlightened female minds, an intuitive perception on these points, by which they may discover almost instantaneously from a look, a tone, a touch responsive to their own, how far it may be desirable to go, and by what shadow they ought to be warned, as well as by what ray of light they ought to be encouraged.

It may be easily imagined how an ignorant, or selfish woman, never can be able to understand all this, and how she may consequently make shipwreck of her husband's happiness, and her own peace, simply from never having known, observed, or felt, what belongs to the nature of the human heart in these its most exquisite touches of light and shade; while, on the other hand, not the highest intellectual attainments, with the noblest gifts of nature, nor all the importance and distinction which these attributes obtain for their possessor in the world, will be able to efface for a moment the delicate perceptions of a truly sensitive woman, or to render her in the deep and fervent love of which she is capable, otherwise than humble, and easily subdued; especially when she comes with childlike simplicity to consult the dial of her husband's love, and to read there the progress of the advancing or receding shadows, which indicate her only true position, through the lapse of every hour.

It is an act of injustice towards women, and one which often brings its own punishment upon talented men, when they select as their companions for life, the ignorant or the imbecile of the other sex, believing that because they are so, they must be more capable of loving. If to be incapable of any thing else, implies this necessity, it must be granted that they are so. But of what value is that love which exists as a mere impulse of nature, compared with that, which, with an equal force of impulse, combines the highest attributes of an enlightened mind, and brings them all with their rich produce, like flowers from a delicious garden, a welcome and appropriate offering at the shrine whereon the heart is laid.

Still I must repeat, that it is not the superiority of talent, but the early and the best use of such as we possess, which gives this power and beauty to affection, by directing it to its appropriate end. For as in other duties of woman's life, without knowledge she cannot, if she would, act properly; so in the expression and bestowment of her love, without an intimate acquaintance with the human heart, without having exercised her faculties of observation and reflection, and without having obtained by early discipline some mastery over her own feelings, she will ever be liable to rush blindly upon those fatal errors, by which the love of married life so often has been wrecked.

In connection with this subject, there is one consideration to which sufficient weight is seldom given; and that is, the importance of never trifling with affection after the nuptial knot is tied. To do this at any time, or in any way, is scarcely consistent with the feelings of a deeply sensitive and delicate mind: but leaving the display of caprice to those who think it gives zest to the familiarity of courtship, it cannot be too deeply impressed upon the female mind, that with the days of courtship it must end.

There are innumerable tests which might be applied to the love of married life, so as to ascertain the degree of its intensity, or the progress of its declension; but who would wish to apply them?—or who, even if they did, would *dare* to make so critical an experiment? If there be any cause for its existence, the consciousness comes soon enough, that the wife is not all to her husband which the flattering promises of early love prepared her to expect; and if there be no cause for the slightest shadow of suspicion that her star is beginning to go down, why trouble her own repose, and that of her husband, by questioning the reality of what it would be worse than death to doubt?

All teasing, all caprice, all acting, for the purpose of renewing an agreeable effect, are therefore inimical to the mutual trust, and the steady confidence in reciprocal affection, which are, or ought to be, enjoyed by individuals thus bound together by an indissoluble tie. Not that the writer would for a moment wish to discountenance that harmless vivacity with which some women know so well how to charm; or to speak of the privacy of married life as consisting of dull and sombre scenes. So far from this, it is her firm belief, that nothing tends more to animate and renew the feeling of affection in the mind of man, than the cheerfulness of his fireside companion.

It is here, then, that the display of native wit and humor may be enjoyed with the greatest zest, for here it is safe; and the husband who comes home to have his spirit refreshed by an easy, natural, and well-timed description of the amusing incidents which have taken place during his absence, will not be the most likely to prefer another fireside to his own.

Even in illness, but especially when laboring only under a slight degree of indisposition, by those who have made cheerfulness a familiar habit, much may be done to prevent the double burden of sickness and sorrow falling upon a husband at once.

There is a vast difference between being as ill as you can be, and as well as you can be. To aim at the latter rather than the former, is the duty of every one, but especially of the married woman, the great business of whose life is to soothe and cheer, not to depress, to weary, or to annoy. If therefore, before marriage, she has been deluded into the notion that a multiplicity of little ailments invested her character with an interesting kind of delicacy; the sooner she becomes perfectly well after marriage, the better it will be for herself, and for all around her.

Lest, however, the liberty of these remarks should appear to touch unkindly those who are *really* afflicted, I must refer the reader for a proof of what may be done in the way of bearing pain with cheerfulness and resignation, to those many beautiful instances which adorn the history of woman, where her own sufferings appear to be forgotten in the intensity of her desire to make others happy. And here again we see the necessity of having made such acts of self-sacrifice habitual. No human being, however great the momentary effort, can practise this kind of self-government, or consistently exercise this degree of generosity, merely from the force of transient impulse; and when the greater claims upon the attention of a wife render illness to her a more painful and trying ordeal than it has ever been before, she will feel the greater need of having practised, in her early years, the habit of so far restraining the expression of personal feeling, as by making the best of her afflictions, and gratefully embracing such opportunities of enjoyment as still remain, to be able to render it not an irksome duty, but a privilege, to be near her in sickness and suffering.

It is a great pity when those trials which render affection so essential to our support, should be made the means of driving it away. Nor is it at all necessary that this should be the case with men; for there is a kindness, and a forbearance, mingled with their higher virtues, which sometimes elicits from them the most devoted and delicate attentions in the season of illness; and all who have experienced, and felt the real value of such attentions, will estimate them too highly, to be willing that a habit of fretful or unnecessary complaining should thus deprive the hour of suffering of its greatest earthly consolation.

It would not be just, even if it were possible, to speak on this subject, and to leave unmarked by expressions of gratitude and admiration, the gentle kindness and untiring patience, with which some men can devote themselves to the duties of a sick-room; or how, by their superior strength, added sometimes to a higher degree of tenderness and delicacy, they can render those services to a weak or suffering wife, which nothing but the love of married life can either purchase or repay. But though one would willingly forgive the wife, who for the gratification afforded by such kindness, would almost wish to suffer, it must ever be remembered, that not by complaining of every little ache and pain, is such kindness to be purchased; but by bearing, with sweetness and serenity, those trials which the all-wise Disposer of human events sees meet to inflict.

It is in seasons such as these, that the perfect identity originating in the marriage bond, is most deeply felt—that identity which gives a spiritual nature to an earthly union. It is true we are told there is no such thing as giving in marriage in heaven; but we are left to enjoy the happiness of believing, that there is something almost heavenly in the "marriage of true minds"—something which brings us nearer, than any other circumstance in this sublunary state, to an apprehension of what must be the enjoyment of those regions of felicity, where all existences are blended into one, and where the essential principle of that one is love.

Nor is it the least wonderful property belonging to this drop of sweetness in life's great ocean, that it can exist almost independently of outward circumstances. How many of the hapless inheritors of poverty and suffering have nothing else; and yet their lot is scarcely to be called bitter, so long as they have this. On the other hand, how many a desolate but jewelled brow, would doff its envied wreath, for the privilege of sharing this enjoyment with one who was equally loving and beloved!

Let us not, however, fall into the romantic notion, that outward circumstances have nothing to do with the maintenance of this strong feeling of identity. Poverty of itself, or privation in the abstract, would probably never be able to shake the foundation of man's love, or woman's either; but such is the complicated texture of the human mind, that no single portion of suffering or enjoyment exists to us alone, but each draws along with it a train of associating links, by which it is connected sometimes with what is most heterogeneous and dissimilar to its own nature. Thus it is the manner in which poverty is borne, which so frequently constitutes the greatest trial of love—the mutual complainings, recriminations, and suspicions, which it calls forth; not its suffering, its destitution, and its abasement, for under these it is within the province of love to support and to console; and, on the other hand, it is the vanity, the dissipation, and the diversity of interests excited by circumstances of extraordinary prosperity, which often prove fatal to the love of married life; when the wider range of duties and privileges, belonging to an exalted station, might have constituted a stronger bond of sympathy between individuals thus elevated together.

Thus the fault is not in the love of married life, that it gives way so often under the trial of outward circumstances; but in the power so frequently brought to bear against it, from·the wrong feelings which circumstances are allowed to call into action.

Of man's love it must ever be remembered too, that if once destroyed, it is destroyed forever. Woman has the strong power of her sympathy and her imagination, by which interest can be re-awakened, and the past can be made to live again; but the nature of man's affection admits of no very potent stimulus from such causes. When once his tenderness toward the object of his affection

is extinguished, his love may too truly be said to have lost its bloom, its freshness, and its intensity. A sense of duty may still supply what propriety requires, and a feeling that his doom is fixed may prevent any great expenditure of thought in sad and unavailing regrets; but who that has looked "on this picture and on that"—who that has observed the dull and leaden aspect presented by married life under these circumstances, could contemplate with equanimity of mind, the possibility of its succeeding in the place of that bright and glowing picture first brought to light by the early promise of mutual love?

It should then be the first and last study of every married woman, to preserve this picture in all its purity, and all its freshness; remembering ever that it is not from the great and stirring accidents of time, that the most danger is to be apprehended; but that sometimes—

"A word unkind or wrongly taken;
  Or Love, which tempest never shook,
  A breath—a touch like this hath shaken."

It is not, therefore, by exemption from outward calamity, that woman can preserve this treasure of her life; but by maintaining through all the little incidents of daily intercourse a true and faithful heart towards her husband—true in its own affections—true also to the various requirements of human nature —and true in its attachment to his interests, both as they relate to time and to eternity.

CHAPTER VII.

TRIALS OF MARRIED LIFE.

IF in describing the domestic happiness of English homes, the love of married life were all which had to be dwelt upon, the task of the writer would be like that of one who enters a garden for no other purpose than to cull the flowers; but as among the fairest productions of nature, the intrusion of noxious weeds must ever be anticipated; so among the brighter scenes of human life, dark passages must occasionally be expected; and happy will it be if they only appear like passing clouds over the landscape, leaving the aspect of the whole more vivid and beautiful, for the trifling interruption to its sameness and repose.

That married life has its peculiar trials, it would imply great ignorance of the actual state of human affairs to attempt to disprove; and while we gladly admit the fact, that it is possible to be happier in this state, than any human being can be alone; we must also bear in mind, that it is possible to be more miserable too—perhaps for this very reason, that the greatest trials connected with this state of existence, are such as cannot be told, and therefore such as necessarily set the sufferer apart from all human sympathy and consolation. Many of these, however, may be greatly ameliorated by a willingness to meet them in a proper way; but more especially, by an habitual subjection of self to the interests and the happiness of others.

Among the trials peculiar to married life, we will first speak of those of temper; and here it is necessary to refer again to the common delusion prevailing among young women, which leads them to look forward to the time of marriage, as the opening of a scene of unlimited indulgence, where every wish will be consulted, and every inclination gratified to its full extent, and where consequently it will be impossible that *offences* should ever come.

It requires but little reflection to perceive, that even if the husband had been sincere in all the promises, which as a lover he held forth, it would not be in his power to render the lot of any woman one of uninterrupted enjoyment; for however faithfully his own part might be fulfilled, it would still be the inevitable consequence of thus setting out together in the serious business of conducting a household, that circumstances should press upon both, so as either to thwart their inclinations, or bend them to submission. Beyond these, however, it must be allowed, that there are no trials of temper arising out of the cross occurrences incident to family af-

fairs, at all to be compared with those which belong to the close intercourse of persons of dissimilar habits bound together for life.

It is a curious fact, that however irritable the temper may be, a stranger has comparatively no power to ruffle it; while, on the other hand, the closer the intimacy, the greater is the liability both to pain and provocation, where that intimacy is made use of as a key to the secret passages of the heart. Hence the bland and patient smiles with which a stranger is sometimes listened to, when a sister or a brother conversing in the same style, would scarcely be endured; and hence the peevish answer sometimes bestowed upon a husband, when a guest is immediately spoken to in the gentlest and most conciliating tone.

There is something, too, in the bare fact of being indissolubly bound together, which, instead of rendering it for that reason an object of supreme desire that the bondage should be one of silken cords, rather than one of weary chains, seems to produce in the human mind, a sort of perverse determination to bear, whatever must be borne, as badly as we can.

That the prospect of having to combat with any trial of temper but for a very limited space of time, has a peculiar effect in rendering it more tolerable, we have sufficient proof in the conduct of hired nurses, who, perhaps, of all human beings, have the most to put up with in the way of provocations of this kind. It cannot be supposed that persons of this description possess any peculiar advantages in the way of mental discipline, to give them this power of self-command; nor is it a question of self-interest, for of all persons, that would be most likely to operate upon the wife; neither have they time or opportunity, in the majority of cases, for attaching themselves by any feelings of affection to the objects of their care. It is the simple fact that all will soon be over, and that to them it is ultimately of no sort of consequence, which enables them to bear with such amazing equanimity the trials of patience to which they are so frequently subjected; while, on the other hand, the consideration that it must be thus, and thus always, appears at once to excite a spirit of resistance where resistance is most vain.

But granting that there is, inherent in the human mind, this spirit of contradiction, and granting also that men, with all their dignified and noble attributes, are sometimes, though often unconsciously, indescribably provoking to an irritable temperament; there is one consideration which a generous mind will be ever willing to dwell upon with so much candor, as at least to make concessions when it has been betrayed into any excess of irritability, if not wholly to submit with cheerfulness and resignation to this peculiar dispensation, regarding it as among the appointments of Providence, designed for purposes inscrutable perhaps to human reason, yet not the less in accordance with mercy, and with wisdom.

But in order to judge more candidly on this subject, let us single out a few instances of the most familiar kind on both sides; and if the merit of unconsciousness, and absence of design, does not preponderate on the side of man, I shall be much mistaken in my calculations.

I have always been accustomed to consider it as the severest trial to the temper of a married woman, to have an idle husband; and if in addition to neglecting his business, or such manly occupations as an exemption from the necessities of business would leave him at liberty to pursue, he is personally idle, sitting slipshod at noontime, with his feet upon the fender, occasionally jarring together the whole army of fire-irons with one stroke of his foot, agitated at intervals by the mere muscular irritation of having nothing to do, or not choosing to do any thing; and if he should happen to have chosen for his wife a woman of active bustling character, as such men not unfrequently do, I believe I must, as in some other instances, leave it to the reader to suggest some possible means by which such a woman may at all times control her temper, and keep the peace at her own fireside.

One thing, however, is certain in such a case—it is not by ebullitions of momentary indignation that an idle man can be stimulated into action. So far from it, he will rather be made worse, and rendered more obstinately idle by any direct opposition to the indulgence of his personal inclinations. Whatever good is to be done in such a case, can only be effected from the convictions of his own mind, brought about by the quiet operation of affectionate and judicious reasoning; for if the wife should be unguarded enough to throw out reproaches against him, representing the disgusting nature of idleness in its true colors; or if she should seek to establish her own claims to his exertions, so as to convey an idea of her arguments tending to a selfish end, she might as well

" — go kindle fire with snow,"

as attempt to rouse her husband into healthy and consistent habits of activity by such means.

Here, too, we might mention as pre-eminent among the trials of married life, though I question whether it operates so immediately upon the temper as some others, the ruinous propensity inherent in the nature of some men, to spend their own money, and sometimes the money of their friends, in vague speculations and visionary schemes.

The man who is possessed with this mania, for in certain cases it deserves no other name, is neither to be convinced by argument nor experience, that after ninety-nine failures, he ·is not very likely to succeed the hundredth time; and the wife who knows that the maintenance of herself and her family is entirely dependent upon him, has abundant need for supplies of strength and patience beyond what any earthly source can afford.

Among other causes of irritation, and forming reasonable ground of complaint, is the disposition evinced by some men to be inconsiderate and cruel to animals; and this I must think, is one of the cases in which we are recommended to *be angry, and sin not.* Yet even in this instance, when we look at the education of boys—and consider the absence there is of all regard to the feelings of animals, even in the minds of the most delicate females, except where early instruction has given to this regard the force of principle—great and charitable allowance ought to be made for the conduct of men in this respect: and perhaps the best and only means of remedying the evil, which any woman can adopt, is to bring up her children, if she be a mother, with higher and more enlightened views of the requirements of Christian duty.

It is a well-known fact, that men in general appear to consider themselves justly entitled to the privilege of being out of humor about their food. Thus the whole pleasure of a social meal is sometimes destroyed by some trifling error in the culinary department, or the non-appearance of some expected indulgence. But here again, our forbearance is called into exercise, by remembering the probability there is, that such men have had silly mothers, who made the pleasures of their childhood to consist chiefly of such as belong to the palate; and here too, if the wife cannot remedy this evil, and in all probability it will be beyond her power to do so, she may, by her judicious efforts to promote the welfare of the rising generation, impart to the youthful minds committed to her care, or subject to her influence, a juster estimate of what belongs to the true enjoyment of intellectual and immortal beings.

With all occasions of domestic derangement, such as washing days, and other renovations of comfort and order, some men of irritable temperament wage open and determined war. But, may we not ask, in connection with this subject, whether their prejudices against these household movements have not been remotely or immediately excited, by the extreme and unnecessary confusion and disturbance with which they are too frequently accompanied? For I cannot think that a reasonable man, on comparing an English home with a French one, for instance, would desire to be altogether exempt from such domestic purifications; and if properly managed, so as to interfere as little as possible with his personal comfort, and conducted with general cheerfulness and good humor, such a man might easily be brought to consider them as necessary to the good of his household, as the refreshing shower is to the summer soil.

A causeless and habitual neglect of punctuality on the part of the master of a house, is certainly a grievance very difficult to bear; because as he is the principal person in the household, and the first to be considered, the whole machinery of domestic management must necessarily be dependent upon his movements; and more especially, since it so happens, that persons who are the most accustomed to keep others waiting, have the least patience to wait for others. Thus it not unfrequently occurs, that a wife is all day urging on her servants to a punctual attention to the dinner-hour appointed by her husband, and when that hour arrives, he has either forgotten it himself, or he allows some trifling hindrance to prevent his returning home until one, or perhaps two, hours later. Yet the same man, though in the habit of doing this day after day, will be excessively annoyed, if for once in his life he should be punctual to the appointed time, and not find all things ready on his return.

Perhaps too the master of a family, on days of household bustle, when extra business has to be done, will not choose to rise so early as usual; or he will sit reading the newspaper while his breakfast waits, and thus keep every member of his family standing about unoccupied, with all the business of the day before them. Or, he may be one of those who like that women should be always ready long before the necessary time, and thus habitually name an hour for meeting, or setting out from home, at which he has not the remotest intention of being ready himself.

Now, as the time of women, if properly employed, is too precious to be wasted, something surely may be done, not by endeavoring to overrule the movements of such a man so as to make him true to his own appointment, but by convincing him, that common honesty requires him simply to state the actual time at which he does intend to be ready. And here we see at once, one of those numerous instances in which a reasonable man will listen, and endeavor to amend; while an unreasonable man will either not listen, or not take the slightest pains to improve.

Again, there are men who like the importance, and the feeling of power and decision which it gives them, to set out on a journey as if upon the spur of the moment, without having communicated their intentions even to the wife, who is most interested in making preparations for such a movement. And there are others, who when consulted about any thing, cannot be brought to give either their attention or their advice, so as to assist the judgment of a wife, who would gladly give satisfaction if she could; yet when the time to act upon their advice is past, will bestow their attention a little too severely upon the unfortunate being, who, consulting her own judgment as the only guide she had, will most probably have done exactly what they did not wish.

But it would be an endless task, to go on enumerating instances of this description. I have merely mentioned these as specimens of the *kind* of daily and hourly trials which most women have to expect in the married state; and which, as I have before stated, may be greatly softened down, if not entirely reconciled, by the consideration already alluded to. Besides which, it is but candid to allow, that the greater proportion of these offences against temper and patience, originate in one of those peculiarities in the character of man which I have omitted to mention in its proper place. I mean the incapability under which he labors, of placing himself in idea in the situation of another person, so as to identify his feelings with theirs, and thus to enter into what they suffer and enjoy, as if the feeling were his own.

This capability appears to be peculiarly a feminine one, and it exists among women in so high a degree, as to leave them little excuse if they irritate or give offence to others; because this innate power which they possess of identifying themselves for the moment with another nature, might, if they would use it for such a purpose, enable them not so much to know, as to feel, when they were giving pain, or awakening displeasure. Men, as I have just stated, are comparatively destitute of this power, as well as of that of sympathy, to which it is so nearly allied. When, therefore, they appear to women so perverse, and are consequently so difficult to bear with, it is often from their being wholly unconscious of the actual state of the case; of the long entanglement of inconveniences which their thoughtless ways are weaving; and consequently of the wounded feeling, disappointment, and vexation, which such thoughtlessness not unfrequently inflicts upon the weaker mind of woman, when the whole framework of her daily existence must be regulated by the movements of a husband who thinks of " none of these things."

But we have not yet sufficiently examined that one consideration, which ever remains to be weighed in the balance against the trials of patience arising out of the conduct of men. And here we must first ask—have you yourself no personal peculiarities exactly opposed to your husband's notions of what is agreeable?—such as habits of disorder, dressing in bad taste, or any other of those minor deviations from delicacy or good breeding, which he might not have had an opportunity of observing before marriage?

We all know that in men these peculiarities are of little importance, compared with what they are in the other sex. If, therefore, you offend in these things, you run imminent risk of impairing, by a succession of little annoyances, the warmth and the intensity of your husband's affection; for man's love, it must ever be remembered, is far more dependent than that of woman, upon having the taste and the fancy always pleased, and consequently upon reposing with perfect complacency on the object of its regard. Have we not all, then, abundant cause to be grateful for being borne with in our infirmities, and loved in spite of our personal defects?

But if such peculiarities as these are of

sufficient importance to cast a shadow over the sunny spots of life, what must we say of some others occasionally observable in the character and conduct of women, to which it is scarcely possible that much charity should be extended? And here I would ask, if you have never treasured up against your husband, some standing cause of complaint, to be thrown at him when an opportunity is offered by the presence of a friend, or a stranger, for discharging this weapon from the household quiver with perfect safety to yourself? Have you not upon the whole preferred having such grievances to complain of, rather than taking such peaceable and judicious measures as would be likely effectually to accomplish their removal?

Have you never, in addition to this, refused an offer of personal gratification when it was convenient or agreeable for your husband to indulge you with it; and professed a somewhat exaggerated desire to accept of it, when the thing was impossible, or at least extremely difficult for your husband to grant?

Have you never made the most of household troubles, spread forth the appurtenances of a wash, allowed the affairs of the kitchen to extend themselves to the parlor, complained unnecessarily of servants and workpeople, and appeared altogether in your own person more harassed, exhausted, and forlorn, after your husband's return home, than you did before, on purpose that he might be compelled, not only to pity you, but to bear a portion of your domestic discomfort himself?

When a concatenation of cross occurrences, hindrances, or mistakes, have rendered every moment one of perplexity and haste; have you never, when involved with your husband in such circumstances, added fuel to the fire by your own petulance, or by your still more provoking exclamations of triumph, that you "thought it would come to that?" Or, when your husband has returned at an hour considerably later than he had appointed, have you never begun with breathless haste to remonstrate with him,

and even allowed your remonstrances to extend to reproaches, before you gave him time to vindicate himself, or to say whether he had not in reality been unavoidably detained?

Now, it is impossible for any woman of right feelings to hide from her conscience, that if she chooses to marry, she places herself under a moral obligation to make her husband's home as pleasant to him as she can. Instead, therefore, of behaving as if it was the great business of married life to complain, it is her peculiar duty as a wife, and one for which, by her natural constitution, she is especially fitted, to make all her domestic concerns appear before her husband to the very best advantage. She has time for her troubles and turmoils, if such things must necessarily be, a fact which I am a little disposed to question, when her husband is absent, or when she is engaged exclusively in her own department; and if she would make his home what it ought to be to him— "an ever-sunny place," she will studiously shield him, as with the wings of love, from the possibility of feeling that his domestic annoyances give weight and poignancy to those more trying perplexities, which most men, engaged either in business, or in public affairs, find more than sufficient for their peace of mind.

By those who write on the subject of temper in connection with the happiness of married life, much is generally said by way of giving weight to the importance of guarding against the *first* angry word. But though it is unquestionably most desirable to keep the tablet of experience as long unsullied as we can, I do not see exactly how this rule applies more to offences of temper, than to any other transgressions of the law of perfect love; for if it be felt, as it must be, a breach of this law to utter an unkind expression; it is equally so to allow any evidence to appear of a disposition to act counter to a husband's wishes, or even to forget or neglect what he considers essential to his comfort.

Indeed, so various are the circumstances to which any remarks upon the subject of temper must apply, that the best possible plan which could be proposed for maintaining harmony and good feeling in one instance, might be the worst in another. As a case in point, there are unquestionably some individuals so constituted, that if in a moment of irritation, they do not speak out, the smothered feeling forcibly pent up, assumes with them the character of sullenness, and even approaches to that of dislike towards the offender. Besides which, we should never know when we did offend, and might consequently go on to the end of life inflicting perpetual annoyance upon our fellow-creatures, if there were no outward evidence of the degree of displeasure which our inadvertences were causing.

Not that I would by any means be guilty of recommending an approach to those violent outpourings of heated and impassioned feeling, which mark out some of the darkest passages of human life, by the remembrance, never to be obliterated, of angry and cruel expressions not possible to be often repeated without destroying the tenderness, and even the very life, of love. What I would say on the other side of the question, is simply this —that in reference to temper, no general rule can be laid down, scarcely can any human aid be called in, because of the diversity of dispositions upon which the influence of temper operates, and the difficulty to mere human reason of discovering exactly what is best for every case. In this, as in every other instance of human frailty, it is the power of religion upon the heart and conduct, which alone can afford any lasting or effectual help.

And after all, as the subject bears upon the affection of human beings one towards another, with creatures frail as we are, and in a state of existence so imperfect as the present, it is not by an exemption from all offences that the purity or the strength of human love can be maintained; but far more so by mutual forgiveness, by sympathy with each other's infirmities, and by the constant exercise of that charity which *thinketh no evil*, and which *suffereth long, and is kind*.

But leaving all further consideration of the trials of temper, as a subject which from its endless variety might rather be made to fill volumes than pages; we must turn to subjects of a more serious and alarming nature, and among these, it cannot be out of place to speak first of the deterioration of a husband's character, as taking precedence of other trials incident to married life.

I have already said there can be no calamity in the vast catalogue of human miseries, at all comparable to watching the gradual extinction of that guiding light from the moral influence of a husband, to which a wife might reasonably be allowed to look for her greatest earthly encouragement in every effort to adhere to the dictates of duty, or the requirements of Christian principle. Here, then, it becomes most important to inquire, what can be done to stem the tide of evil, before it shall have borne away the whole fabric of domestic happiness.

A true-hearted woman, herself impressed with the importance of moral and religious principle, will ever be most studious of her husband's safety in this respect; and if her own character, and her own example, are such as to give weight to her remonstrances, there is no calculating the degree to which her influence may not extend. Women, too, are often remarkably quick-sighted to the minor shades of good and evil; and they are thus sometimes enabled to detect a lurking tendency to what is wrong, before the mind of man is awakened to suspicion. Even in business, then, and in all affairs in which men are most liable to be deluded by self-interest, and by the prevailing customs of the world, and thus are too frequently betrayed into transactions at variance with the spirit, if not with the letter, of the law of just and honorable dealing; a right-minded woman may sometimes so place before her husband the affair in which he is engaged, as to make him see at once the error into which he might have fallen; and having seen this clearly, she may possibly enjoy the satisfaction of beholding him adopt, throughout his intercourse with others, a more strict and equitable rule of action.

As this subject, however, in its highest and

most serious import, belongs more properly to a subsequent chapter, we will consider more especially two particular defects in the moral character of men, which may be truly said, wherever they exist, to constitute the severest and most painful trials of married life.

The first of these is intemperance; and here I am aware that my own views on this subject are scarcely such as ought to occupy a place in this work; not because I could not earnestly recommend them to the adoption of every English wife, but because, to do them ample justice, I should be compelled to fill a volume.

Intemperance, then, to treat it as a common vice, should, like every other evil tendency, be watched in its commencement; and here the eye of a conscientious and devoted wife will be far better able to detect the mischief, than his, who, perhaps, in the secret of his heart, would rather not behold it even if he could. I believe there is no difficulty to a delicate-minded person, equal to that of warning a beloved friend or relative of his danger in this respect, else why do we see so many hundreds—nay, thousands looking on, and not stretching out a helping hand until it is too late?

The fact is, that if impressed in any common measure with a sense of justice or of generosity, we cannot do it, so long as we ourselves pursue the same course, only not exactly to the same extent. We cannot look into the face of a familiar friend, and say—"If you take one glass more, you will be guilty of a vulgar and degrading sin; while I, by taking one glass less, commit no sin at all." And it must come to this, where it is the degree, and not the act itself, which constitutes the evil. It must come to the smallest possible measurement, to mark that minute, and ever shifting line, which separates an act allowed and sanctioned by the wise and good, from one which stamps a human being with infamy in this world, and deprives him of all title to admission into the blessedness of the world to come.

Leaving it then to women whose hearts might have animated the wives of Sparta, if the absence of all sympathy and tenderness for the weak in their weak points, may rank among the characteristics of those heroines of the past—leaving it to such women to sit down every day to an indulgence, which in a mere trifle of extent beyond their own measure of gratification, they would deny to a husband—I must candidly confess, that I am wholly at a loss to know what to advise, should that husband, advancing a little and a little further by imperceptible degrees, at last exceed the bounds of strict propriety, and finally hasten on towards the "drunkard's grave."

It is said again and again of such men, that they ought to stop in time; but which is the time? It may vary according to the state of their own health, as well as with the nature of the refreshment of which they partake; while with no two individuals will it ever be found exactly the same. Besides which, it must always be remembered, that the right time to stop, is the time when the intemperate man least wishes to do so; because in exact proportion to his danger, has been his inability to perceive it, and his increase of inclination to go onward towards excess.

Tell me then, ye wise and potent reasoners on this subject, who hold yourselves above the vulgar error of believing that total abstinence is the only safe and efficient means of rescuing the tempted man from ruin,—tell me, or rather tell the afflicted wife, what I am utterly unequal to, by what means she is to conquer, or even to restrain, the habit of intemperance in her husband, except by inducing him altogether to abstain, and by abstaining altogether herself.

One remark, however, may not be inappropriate here, as it applies equally to the point of view in which the subject has so long been held by the world in general, and to that in which it is the happier privilege of some in the present day to behold it. I mean that a husband should never be made the subject of reproach for transgressions of this nature. If he be a man of feeling, his spirit will be sufficiently wounded by a sense of his own degradation; and if not, he will only be hardened by such treatment, and driven, as a means of revenging himself, into still greater excess.

Indeed, nothing but the utmost delicacy, forbearance, and gentleness, will ever be found to answer in such a case; and whatever means are employed, they must be confined in their operation to seasons of perfect sanity, and especially reserved for those occasions of fitful penitence, which often succeed to the most extravagant indulgence; when, partly from the weakness of an exhausted frame, and partly from the satiety of inclination, the victim of intemperance will sometimes throw open his heart to a confidential friend, whose kind and judicious treatment of him at such times, may not improbably be rendered conducive to his ultimate recovery.

Here, too, much may be done by making his home all that it ought to be to a husband, by receiving him on his return with cordial smiles, by amusing him with pleasant conversation, but, more than all, by exercising over him, in a mild and prudent manner, that influence which it is the high privilege of a loved and trusted wife to attain.

Could all women who encourage their husbands in the commencement of intemperance, not only by smiling with evident satisfaction at any extraordinary proofs of good humor or excitement as they begin to appear, but beyond this, and far more effectually, by their own example—could all such women " look to the end," and see the bitter fruits of this trifling with the serious indications of a growing evil, they would stand appalled at the magnitude of their own sufferings, in having to watch from day to day, through their future lives, the gradual extinction of all they had ever loved in the being to whom they must still be united. They would see then how the very countenance may lose its beauty, and like some hideous form that grows upon us in a feverish dream, assume first one aspect of distortion, and then another, until all trace becomes extinct of the " divinity" that stirred "within." They would see then

what an awful wreck is that presented by a lost and polluted mind; and they would feel, in all its reality, what it is to be desolate and alone. For the woman thus circumstanced must not complain. She must not ask for sympathy, for that would be to expose the folly and disgrace of him, about whom her hopes still linger; over whose degraded brow she would still fondly spread the soft shadow of her tenderness, that no ray of piercing light might reach it, to render more conspicuous its deformity and its shame. No; she can only lock her griefs within her own bosom, and be still.

It must be from ignorance, for the phenomenon is not to be accounted for in any other way than on the ground of ignorance of what is to be found in human life, as well as what is the capability of the human heart for suffering and enjoying, which leads so many kindly-disposed and well-intentioned women into such culpable neglect of points connected with this important subject.

One would willingly believe it was because they had never, even in idea, realized what it must be to live through one long night of anxious expectation, when the crisis of a husband's fate had come, and when that single night would decide whether he had sufficient mastery over himself to resist, or whether he would allow his inclination to lead him for the last time over the barrier, and finally to plunge himself and his helpless family into irremediable wretchedness and ruin.

It is in such seasons as these, that every moment is indeed an age, and every pulse like an advancing or receding wave, which falls with heavy swell upon the shore of life. And then what sharpening of the outward senses!—what quickening of the ear to distant sounds, giving to that which lives not, a vitality, until the very step is heard, and then —another wave of the fast-ebbing tide, and all is gone, and all is silent as before. The eye, too, though dim with tears, and wearied out with watching, what does it not behold! —creating out of " strange combinations" of familiar things, some sudden and unexpected

:e that he has returned! Yes, already
Then follows an instantaneous flash
reproach for having judged him with
:le kindness. But, no; the vision
way, and with it sinks the heart of the
dulous believer.

if such be the quickening of the out-
:nses, what must be that of the differ-
culties of the mind?—of memory,
cruel task it is through those long
hours, to paint the smiling past, to
it live again with such intensity of
:ss, that while no actual form intrudes,
ual sound breaks through the chain of
t, the phantasy grows real; and old
:ions wake again, and voices speak
ly, and cordial looks, and gentle loving
·e interchanged, and pure soft feelings
s each other, as in those early days
he sweet "trysting time" was kept,
·pe made light of expectation. Oh,

It is a dream—a very dream.
rorse—the vision of the sleeper may
, but this can never—never live

e is no credulity like that of love.
er dark may be the fear which alter-
vith hope in the mind of her who is
:uated, she has, under all, and support-
: through all the deep foundation of
n unchanging love—that love which
g *as death*. And by the same com-
:ive rule, which to her includes in one
nion every faculty and feeling of her
·y this rule she judges of her husband,
culates the probability of his return.
rule it is impossible that he should
her prayers, and her entreaties, her
, her suffering, and her tears. By
e, then, he must of necessity remem-
in that gay circle, even when its mirth
revelry are at their height. She has
:d him—deeply wronged him, to think
ld forget. Another hour will find him
side, repaying, Oh, how richly! all
:ious fears.

1 these sweet thoughts, she rises and
·er fire again, and draws her husband's
eside the hearth, bethinking her, with

joyous recollection, of some other little acts
of kindness by which she may possibly be
able to make his home look more attractive.
But still he comes not; and that strange sickness of the heart begins again, and creeps
along her frame, until her very fingers ache
with anguish; and tremblingly her hands are,
clasped together, and were it not for prayer,
her heart would surely break with its strong
agony; for still he comes not. Yet,—slowly
as the heavy hours drag on, the midnight
chime at last is heard, that solemn peal, which
tells to some its tale of peace, of safety, and
of home; while it speaks to others but of
darkness, desolation, and despair.

But who shall fill from one sad moment to
another the page of busy thought, or paint
the ever-shifting scenes which flit before the
lonely watcher's mind? Another hour, and
still he comes not.—Yet hark! It is his step
—She flies to meet him—Let us close a scene
for which earth holds no parallel; for here
are mingled, horror, shame, repulsion and
contempt, with a soft tenderness like that of
some sad mother for her idiot child—joy that
the shrouding wings of love once more can
shelter him—bliss that no other eye but hers
is there to see—kind yearning thoughts of
care to keep him in his helplessness from
every touch of harm—feelings so gentle, yet
so powerful, of a strange gladness to be
near him in his degradation—to press the
hand which no one else in the wide world
would hold—to kiss the brow which has no
trace of beauty left! And to do this, night
after night—to live through all the changes
of this scene, through months and years, only
with less of hope, and more of anguish and
despair!

Such is the picture not exaggerated, for
that would be impossible, of one short portion
in the experience of how many women! We
cannot number them. They are to be met
with in society of every grade, and yet society for the most part can rest satisfied to do
nothing more than pity them. Nor scarcely
that; for the same voice which speaks with
feeble lamentations of the suffering of the
wife, will often press the husband to the fes-

tive board, and praise the sparkling wine, and urge him to partake.

But it is time to turn our attention to the contemplation of another of the trials of married life, of which it is to be hoped that few who read these pages, will have any cause to think with reference to themselves. It may be said, "Why then remind them of the possibility that such causes of trial may, or do, exist?" I answer, that although the extreme of the case to which I am about to allude, is, happily for us, comparatively seldom known among respectable families in the middle ranks of life in England; yet, there are degrees of proximity to these extremes, existing sometimes where we should least expect to find the cheerful aspect of domestic life cast under such a cloud.

In reflecting seriously and impartially upon the love of married life, we must all be forcibly impressed with the fact, that the love which is most frequently presented to the notice of the observer, is far from being such as we ourselves should be satisfied to possess; or, at all events, not such as women of deep and sensitive feelings would expect to meet with in the married state. It is true, there are instances, and they can scarcely be dwelt upon with too much admiration, where the love of married life, in all its imperishable beauty, outlives the bloom of youth, and sheds a radiance like the sunset glow of evening, around the peaceful passage of old age towards the tomb. And were it not that in such instances, we see the possibility of earthly love being kept in all its vigor and its freshness, uninjured by the lapse of time, it would be useless to follow up the inquiry every married woman ought to make—by what means is this love to be preserved?

If in speaking of the peculiar trial about to occupy our attention, I use the word unfaithfulness, to signify my meaning, it is less in reference to those extremes of moral delinquency which sometimes stain the history of private, as well as public life, than to those slighter shades of the same character, which more frequently flit across the surface of domestic peace; or, what is still more lament-

able, remain to cloud the atmosphere of home-enjoyment, until the whole experience of married life becomes as dull, and soulless, and devoid of interest, as if the union was simply one of habit or convenience, endured with mutual indifference, yet dragged on with decency and something like respect, because it was "so nominated in the bond."

But is it right that creatures endowed with capabilities for the highest and holiest enjoyment, should be satisfied with this? Nay, is it possible that happiness of so low a grade, if one may call it such, can fill the heart whose quick susceptibilities, whose trembling emotions, and whose living depths, have been formed to answer, and to echo every touch and tone of feeling, from the highest thrill of ecstasy, down to the lowest notes of wo? No: if we are reckless how we turn from its high destiny, a nature thus endowed; if we will thus sink the immortal in the material, so as merely to work out with mechanical precision the business of each day, in which the animal nature holds pre-eminence over the spiritual, we must not venture to complain that life is vapid and monotonous, or that there is little in this world to remind us of that blessedness which is promised as the portion of the happy in the next.

Whatever we aim to possess as a privilege even in this life, let it then be of the highest order; and having attained our wish, let us seek to preserve that privilege unimpaired. That which elevates the soul in its capability of enjoyment, is always worthy of our care; while that which lowers it, is always to be shunned and feared. In nothing is this more important to be observed, than in the preservation of earthly love. That which degrades the standard of affection, degrades the whole being; and that which raises this standard, raises also every faculty which can be connected either immediately or remotely with the exercise of the affections.

I have already described, in some particulars, how that best gift of Providence, the love of a faithful and devoted husband, is to be preserved. We have now the painful task of supposing that it has been allowed, by some means or other, to fall away. There are faint and frequent symptoms of this decline, of which the judgment takes no cognizance, until after the heart has been made to feel them; and although I have already alluded to the folly and the danger of voluntarily looking out for such symptoms where there is no reason to suppose they exist, there may be equal, if not greater danger, in disregarding them where they do.

I will only mention as the first of these symptoms, an increased tendency on the part of the husband to be repelled or annoyed by little personal peculiarities. And here it may be observed, that almost every impression injurious to the love of man in married life, is personal or immediate, rather than remote. Thus a husband will more easily forgive his wife for an act of moral culpability, provided it has no reference to himself, than for the least personal affront, or the slightest occasion for even a momentary sensation of disgust. It consequently happens, that when affection begins to wane, the husband often becomes annoyed with the voice, the manner, the dress of his wife, more than he is with those of other women. She has, then, some peculiar way of doing every thing which seems to jar upon his senses; and in time he ceases so entirely to look, to listen, or to linger near her, that unless more than commonly obtuse, she must be made to feel that she has lost her power to charm him, and when that is lost—alas, for the poor wife!

Still we must not forget, that there are two kinds of unfaithfulness, the one arising entirely from estranged affection; and the other from attraction towards a different object. In the latter case it does not always follow that affection for the wife shall have become extinct, and therefore there is hope; but, in the former, the fact that man's love when once destroyed is destroyed forever, excludes all possibility of consolation, except from a higher and a surer source. As well might the mourner weeping for the dead, expect by tears and lamentations to reanimate the lifeless form; as the unloved wife to recall the affection of her husband, after the bloom and

tenderness of his love is gone. Who then would incur the risk of so vast and irreparable a loss, by a neglect of those personal attractions by which it was her study in early life to charm? Who would allow a careless or negligent demeanor to impress her husband's mind with the conviction, that he was not in her estimation of sufficient importance to make it worth her while to please? or who would be willing that the powers of her mind should fall into disuse, when they might in their happiest and yet most natural exercise, be made conducive to the one great end of increasing her husband's interest in his home?

To feel herself an unequal companion to the being whom of all others she would most wish to please, to have never cultivated her powers of conversation, and to be conscious that her society is vapid and uninteresting, must be one of the most painful and humiliating feelings to which an amiable woman can be subject: but to see, what is very natural in such a case, that others have a power which she has not, to call forth the higher faculties of her husband's mind, to elevate his thoughts, to charm his fancy, and to enliven his spirits!—Surely if the daughters of England could realize by any exercise of their imagination, the full intensity of feelings such as these, they would cease to be careless about the cultivation of those means of promoting social and domestic happiness, with which every woman who enters upon the duties of a wife, ought to make herself acquainted.

But beyond this vague and general feeling of being neglected, and this incapacity for doing any thing to avert so desolate a doom, it sometimes happens that there is real cause to suspect a transfer of the husband's interest and affection to another. And although nothing can be more destructive to the happiness of married life, or more at variance with the nature of true and deep affection, than a predisposition to suspicion on these points; yet where the case is too evident to admit of doubt, it would evince a culpable indifference in the wife who could suffer it to remain unnoticed.

Here, however, if ever in the whole range of human experience, it is necessary to act with delicacy and caution. It is necessary, in the first place, to be sure. In the next, no selfish motive, no indignant feeling, no disposition to revenge, must mingle with what is said or done on so melancholy and momentous an occasion; for though the dignity of virtue, and the purity of the female character, as well as the temporal and eternal good of the offender, alike require that some decided measures should be adopted to avert the evil; the wife herself must not forget, that under such circumstances she possesses no other than a legal claim—that, as a being to be cherished and beloved, she is utterly discarded from her husband's heart—that scarcely is his home her own—that her respectability, her position in society, all that in which an honored and a trusted wife delights, are only nominally hers; and that she is in reality, or rather, in all which belongs to the true feelings of a woman, a low, lost thing, more lonely, pitiable, and degraded, than the veriest outcast from society who still retains a hold upon her husband's love. What, then, are admiration, wealth, or fame, to such a woman? Society, even though she were its idol, would have no power to flatter her; nor could the wide world, with all its congregated millions, awake within her desolate bosom a single thrill of pride. No, there is nothing but uncomplaining loneliness, and utter self-abasement, for the portion of that wife who cannot keep her husband's heart!

It is in this spirit alone, that with any propriety or any hope, she can appeal to a husband's feelings, carefully guarding against all expression of tenderness, no longer welcome or desired; and keeping, as it were, aloof in her humility; yet withal, casting herself upon his pity, as one who is struck down by a beloved hand, will kiss the instrument of her abasement; putting aside all selfish claims, as indeed she must; and making it evident, that though her own happiness is wrecked for ever, she cannot live without a hope, nor breathe without a prayer, for him.

And surely, if all this is carried out to the full extent of woman's delicacy, disinterestedness, and truth; and if accompanied by earnest and unceasing prayer for that help which no human power can then afford—surely, towards a wife thus suffering and sincere, the husband whose heart is not yet wholly depraved, could scarcely withhold his pity, his protection, and his love!

And if the husband should relent, if he should renounce the object of attraction to his wandering fancy, though nothing can obliterate the past, or break the chain of association between that and the thousand apprehensions which must of necessity link themselves into the sad future; all these dark thoughts must be concealed within her bosom, into whose secret counsels, and more secret griefs, no earthly friend must be admitted. Neither must sadness cloud her brow, nor any lurking suspicion betray itself upon the smooth surface of her after-life, but vivacity and cheerfulness again must charm; while a manner disengaged, and a mind at liberty to please, and receive pleasure in return, must prove the mastery of principle over impulse—of affection over self.

If with a wife thus circumstanced, the power to forget should appear the greatest mercy a kind Providence could bestow; and if this mercy being denied, the aspect of her life should look too dark to be endured, she must not forget that one earthly consolation yet remains—it is that of having kept her own affection unchanged and true: and oh! how infinitely preferable is the feeling of having borne unfaithfulness than of having been unfaithful ourselves!

But beyond, and far above such consolation, is that of being remembered in her lost and low estate, by Him who *chasteneth whom he loveth;* of being permitted in her degradation to come and offer up her broken heart to Him; when deprived of every other stay, to call Him father, and to ask in humble faith the fulfilment of His gracious promise of protection to those who put their trust in Him.

CHAPTER VIII.

POSITION IN SOCIETY.

In a previous work, addressed to the "Daughters of England," I have proposed as the first serious inquiry of a thinking mind, that all young persons entering upon the active duties of life, should ask this question—what is my actual position? And if in the season of early youth this question is important, it is equally, if not more so, immediately after marriage, especially as the position of a woman must always depend upon that of her husband, where society is so constituted that a man may raise or lower his wife, though no woman, except in very peculiar cases, can effect any material alteration in the rank or station of her husband.

Thus it is highly important, in taking upon herself the duties of a new home, that the wife should ascertain precisely what is her position with regard to those with whom she associates; for there is as great a deviation from good sense, integrity, and right feeling, in being servile to the great, as in being haughty to the poor.

But it is impossible to enter upon this subject, without being afresh reminded of one of those inconsistencies which mark the general tone of feeling and habit in society of the middle ranks in England. I mean a striking inequality between the degree of refinement, self-indulgence, and luxury, existing among men, and that which is generally found among women of the same rank. In families whose dependence is entirely upon business, this is especially the case, at least in our large towns and cities; for, while the sons are sent out at an early age, to engage in all the drudgery of the shop or the warehouse, the daughters remain at home, not unfrequently the occupants of elegant drawing-rooms, with little else to do than practise their music lessons, manufacture their wax-flowers, or pursue, according to the popular notions of the day, those various and infallible methods of renovating a feeble constitution, which, in nine cases out of ten, in reality wants nothing more than a little wholesome activity to render it as strong as either happiness or usefulness require.

Now, though it is far from the wish of the writer to wage war against any of those ingenious occupations which fill up the spare time of young ladies in general, provided such occupations are kept in their proper place, and made to fill up *spare* time only; yet, against the morbid feelings both of mind and body, which are engendered by a life of mere trifling, all who wish well to the sex, both in this and other countries, must feel it a sacred duty to use such influence as they possess.

It is, however, the foolish pride, and the false notions of what is, or is not, becoming, naturally arising out of the state of existence to which our young *ladies* of the middle class of society in England are consigned, which, more than any thing else, interfere with their happiness, and prevent their being in reality either a help, or a comfort, to the companions whose lot they are bound to share for life.

England as a nation has little to boast of beyond her intellectual and her moral power. It is in this that her superiority is felt and acknowledged by the world; and in this it might almost be allowed her to indulge a sort of honest pride. That this power is chiefly lodged with the middle classes, I think all have agreed; and that, originating in them, it is made to operate more extensively through the efficient instrumentality of a comparatively well-ordered and wisely governed population of working people.

What then would England gain individually or collectively, by the middle classes aspiring upwards to imitate the manners, and adopt the customs of the aristocracy? No; let her shopkeepers be shopkeepers still—her farmers, farmers—and the wives and daughters of such honest, manly, and honorable citizens of the world, let them no longer blush to owe the comfort of their homes to the profits of a well-conducted trade.

To say nothing of the want of right submission to the will of Providence, evinced by being foolishly above the situation we are born to; it is in my opinion a sort of rebellion, or rather treachery, against the welfare of our country, to be thus unwilling to maintain, what future ages will agree to have been the glory of the times in which we live.

Besides which, it requires but little knowledge, but little observation of society in other countries, and but little acquaintance with the world in general, to see that those distinctions which give to one occupation so much more dignity than another, must be purely conventional. Let us look, as an instance of this, at the vast difference we make in our notions of gentility between wholesale and retail business. And though a man of noble birth, as he drives by necessity through the bustling streets of London, would smile at the idea that trade was not a degradation of itself sufficient to exclude all notion of degree; yet the tradesman living at his shop knows perfectly well, that his wife and daughters have no right to visit with the wife and daughters of him who keeps his country house, and sells *en masse*, from some dark warehouse in the city, the self-same articles in which the other deals.

Still these distinctions, strongly and clearly as they are occasionally impressed upon the inferior classes, become sometimes a little intricate, as wealth enables its possessor to advance in the scale of luxury and indulgence. When the city shopkeeper, for instance, obtains sufficient to enable him to settle in his rural villa, from whence he issues every morning to his counting-house in town, the wife and daughters who remain to set the fashions of the village where they live—how immeasurably far are they from holding intercourse with any of the shopkeepers there! Even when affairs connected with the welfare of the neighborhood render it necessary to call upon the shopkeeper's wife, they meet her in a manner the most distant, and the most unlike what could by any possibility be construed into friendship.

But in order to see more clearly the perfect absurdity of such distinctions, we have only to make a sudden transition of thought to the state of a new colony, on some uncivilized and distant shore ; and ask what difference any one would think of making there, between the member of that little community who should prepare the skins of wild animals for general use, and him who should manufacture such skins into articles of wearing apparel ? or who would pronounce upon the inferiority of occupation in him who should employ himself each day in catering for a single meal, to that of him who should, in a longer space of time, provide for many meals together ?

That the man who held the reins of government over such a community, would merit some distinction, I am free to allow, because his situation would be one to which he must have risen either by his own superiority of mind, or by the unanimous consent of the rest, who agreed, at the time they appointed him to the office, to evince towards him the respect which is always due to influence rightly exercised. In the same manner, and according to their different degrees of capability, many of the others would, no doubt, work their way to offices of responsibility and trust, instituted for the good of the whole body, and each entitled to its share of respect and confidence. But that working in one material more than another, handling one article of food or apparel, or even dealing in a large or a small way, with those who buy and sell, should be able to create distinctions of such importance as to separate society into mere fractions, or to invest one party with honor, and cast odium upon the other, is a phenomenon which has been left for the enlightened stage of civilization in which we live, fully to develop, though the march of intellect has hitherto failed to reduce the whole to a system, so as to be understood and acted upon with any degree of certainty and precision.

It may be said, and perhaps with too much truth, that the business of shopkeeping, as it is generally conducted, has little tendency to ennoble the character ; and that perpetually striving to please for purposes of self-interest, those who in reality are sometimes cordially despised, is lowering to the dignity of a man, to say nothing of a gentleman.

It may be asked, on the other hand, who, in the present state of society, is exempt from this particular kind of degradation? The lawyer, who may be said almost to hold the destinies of his fellow-creatures in his hand—he cringes to his wealthy client, and often works his way to distinction by concealing his real sentiments, and pretending to be other than he is. The doctor, too, with his untiring patience, and his imperturbable serenity, approaching with apparent kindness and respect, where every feeling of his soul is repelled—who would speak of him as an independent man, more especially in the outset of his career? Nor is this less the case with other professions, all which, however, are esteemed more honorable, and consequently more eligible, than any kind of trade. But still—

"A man's a man for a' that;"

and let his occupation be what it may, it is the honest heart, the upright principle, the steady mind, and the unbiased judgment, which give him dignity wherever he may be placed. The man who possesses these qualifications, in addition to a far-stretching and enlightened intellect, must ever be a pillar to the state in which he lives, for he will uphold its integrity, and without such men no nation can be truly great.

As the chosen companion of such a man, is it possible, then, that an English woman born to the same rank in society, should blush to acknowledge herself a tradesman's wife? Nor is this all. It is not the bare acknowledgment that she is so, which can in any way be made to answer the demands of duty, but a perfect willingness to adapt herself in every respect to her situation, so as to answer its various requirements to the satisfaction of all around her. And here the sisters who have been separated so widely from their brothers in the formation of their social and domestic habits, are found so often and so lamentably at fault; not always because they are unwilling to do what duty may require, but because from having early imbibed false notions of what is really honorable, and really degrading, they do their duty, if at all,

in a troubled, fretful, and discontented spirit, as much at variance with what a husband would naturally desire in the companion of his home, as with what ought to be exhibited as the graces of the Christian character.

Yet what can be expected of such wives, for they have their sickly sensibilities arising out of the false position they have held, and for which they have been training; they have the romance engendered by indolence and light reading; they have the love of self, which personal indulgence has strengthened into a habit; they have their delicate constitutions, and their thousand ailments—they have all these to contend with, and all operating powerfully against the cheerful performance of the new duties in which they are involved.

Who can have witnessed the situation of such women in their married state, without longing to awaken the whole sisterhood to a different estimate of duty, and of happiness? Who can have observed their feeble striving after nobler effort, when too late to attain the power of making it to any useful purpose—the spirit broken, the health impaired, the beauty and vivacity of youth all gone; the few accomplishments upon which their time was wasted, forgotten, or remembered only as a dream; the wish without the hope to do better for the future, than has been done for the past, the failing of pecuniary means, resources gradually diminishing in proportion to the increase of demand—sickness, servants, children, and their education, all requiring more and more—who that has ever looked upon all this, and there are not a few among the boasted homes of England where the reality of this picture might be found, would not yearn with aching heart over so lamentable a waste of good feeling and intention, arising solely out of the early, but wrong basis of the female mind with regard to common things?

But let us not despair. Where ignorance and not perverseness constitutes the foundation of any prevailing evil, the whole may easily be remedied. Let us look then again at the constitution of English society, at the vast proportion of good which is effected by the middle classes, at the mass of intellect it comprehends, at the genius by which it is adorned, at the influence it commands, at the dignity with which it is invested by the state, and last, but not least, at its independence; for if, on the one hand, it claims exemption from the necessary hardships and restrictions of the poor, on the other, it is equally privileged in its exemption from the arbitrary requirements of exalted rank.

It is unquestionably one of the great advantages of being born to this station, that we are comparatively free to think and act for ourselves; that our heritage is one of liberty, with the rational enjoyment of which no one has a right to interfere. We have our intellectual privileges, too, and leisure for the cultivation of the mind; our social meetings, where we dare to speak the honest feelings of the heart, no man being able to make us afraid; our hospitality unshackled by the cold formalities of rank; our homes supplied with every comfort, and it may be, adorned with elegance; our fireside pleasures uninterrupted; our ingatherings of domestic joy sacred to those who dwell beneath the same protecting roof; and no interference with our sentiments, or our religion, but each one left to follow out the purpose of a merciful Creator, by choosing his Bible and his conscience as his only guide.

And what could any reasonable woman wish for more? Or having found herself a member of a community thus constituted, why should she reject its noble privileges, for the sake of any feeble hold she may obtain of such as belong more probably to another, and a higher sphere?

I have already stated, in an earlier portion of this work, that true dignity can only be maintained by adaptation to our circumstances, whatever they may be: thus there can be no dignity in assuming what does not belong to our actual position in society; though many temptations to fall into this error are placed in the way of women in general. When, for instance, the wife of a respectable tradesman is associated with persons of superior rank in the duties of private or public charity, she is frequently treated with a degree of kindness and freedom, which, if not on her guard against the fascinating manners of that class of society, might easily beguile her into the belief that no real difference of rank was felt to exist. But just in proportion as she would herself desire to be affable and kind to those beneath her, without such kindness being presumed upon as an evidence of equality; so it often happens that ladies of rank do really enjoy a certain degree of friendly and social intercourse with women of good sense occupying a lower station, when at the same time they would shrink away repelled by the least symptom of the difference of rank being forgotten by the inferior party.

It is the instinct of natural delicacy then which leads us rather to withdraw our familiarity, than to have it withdrawn from; and if thus sensible of what is her proper sphere, and scrupulous to observe its limits, a right-minded woman need never be made to feel that she is not respected; although the moment she steps beyond the boundary of that sphere, the true dignity of her character will be gone.

Nor is this the case with her position in society alone. All misapprehensions about herself, such as supposing she is beautiful when she is not, or highly gifted when no evidence of talent appears, or important when she has no influence—all these mistakes are calculated to deprive a woman of that dignity which is the inalienable possession of all who fill with perfect propriety their appointed place.

It is scarcely necessary in the present state of society to point out, on the other hand, the loss of character and influence occasioned by living below our station; for if in some individual minds there is an inherent tendency to sink and grovel in their own sphere, or to be servile and cringing to those above them; such a propensity forms so rare an exception to the general character of the times in which we live, as scarcely to need any further comment, more especially as such a disposition is exposed by its own folly to that contempt which constitutes its proper punishment.

It is, however, deeply to be regretted, that often where this tendency is not inherent, nor consequently a part of individual character, it has in too many instances been induced by the severe and constant pressure of pecuniary difficulties, rendering it an act of necessity, rather than of choice, that the favor of the distinguished or the wealthy should be sought, and their patronage obtained, as the only means of ensuring success, and sometimes as the only hope of preserving a helpless family from want or ruin.

Pitiable as this situation may be, and frequent as there is every reason to fear it is, much may be done in cases of this kind to keep up the moral dignity of a husband and a family, by the influence of a high-principled wife, who will make it the study of her life to prove that it is not in the power of circumstances to degrade an upright and independent mind.

If, then, it is a duty of paramount importance for a wife to ascertain what is her exact position in society, and to endeavor to adapt herself to it wherever it may be; her next duty is to consider well the *manner* of doing this. We can all feel, in the case of our servants and dependents, the vast difference there is between a willing and an unwilling service. How striking then must be this difference, where all the social affections, and the best feelings of the heart, are implicated, as they must be, in the conduct of a wife!

I can think of no more appropriate word by which to describe the manner in which her duties ought to be performed, than the homely phraseology we use, when we speak of things being done *heartily;* for it is precisely in this way that she may most effectually prove to her husband how entirely she considers her destiny, with all its hopes, and all its anxieties, to be identified with his. As a mere matter of policy, too, nothing can be more likely to ensure the happiest results, since whatever we do *heartily,* produces in one sense its own reward, by stimulating in-

to healthy activity the various powers of the mind and body, and thus exciting a degree of energy and cheerfulness, alike calculated to enhance the pleasure of success, or to support under the trial of disappointment. While on the other hand, a shrinking, reluctant, halfish way of falling in with the requirements of duty, by perpetuating the sensation of self-sacrifice, and dragging out each individual effort into a lingering and painful struggle, is not more likely to produce the most unfavorable impression upon the minds of those with whom we are associated, than to weary out our own inclination to do right, at the same time that it effectually destroys our happiness and our peace of mind.

I have thus far, in relation to position in society, spoken only of cases in which the wife may be liable to feel that her situation is a humiliating one, and I have been compelled to do this at some length—from the fact already noticed, of the sisters in families connected with business, being generally so far in advance of their brothers, not only as regards their notions of what is suitable or becoming to themselves, but also the habits they have cultivated of refinement and personal indulgence, as to render it scarcely possible for them to marry in the same sphere of life, without having much to endure before they can enter with full purpose of heart into all the requirements of their new situation.

But if cases of this kind constitute the majority of those which fall under our notice, we must not forget that in English society, it is the privilege of many persons in the middle ranks to be placed in circumstances of affluence and ease, where the luxuries of life, and even its elegances, may properly be enjoyed. And if the first aspect of such a lot should present the idea of greater personal indulgence being its lawful accompaniment; on the other hand, the serious and reflecting mind must be struck with the important fact, that in proportion to more extensive means of enjoyment, must be a wider influence, and a greater amount of responsibility.

To use this influence aright, and to render

to her conscience a strict account of these responsibilities, will be no light undertaking to the English wife; and as we live, happily for us, in a country where channels are perpetually opened for our benevolence, and opportunities perpetually offered for our efforts to do good, we cannot, if we would, rest satisfied with the plea, that our disposition towards usefulness meets with no field for its development.

It so happens, however, that the same position in society which presents such facilities for the exercise of better feeling, presents also innumerable temptations to the gratification of female vanity, indolence, and self-indulgence, with all the evils which commonly follow in their train. The very title of this chapter—"Position in Society,"—where it conveys an idea of wealth and influence, never fails to conjure up a host of enemies to simple Christian duty, some of which are so deceptive and insidious, as effectually to escape detection, until their magnitude, as plants of evil growth, becomes a cause of just alarm.

The great facility with which the elegances and luxuries of life are now obtained, and the general competition which prevails throughout society with regard to dress, furniture, and style of living, present to a vain and unenlightened woman, an almost irresistible temptation to plunge into that vortex of extravagance, display, and worldly-mindedness, in which, I believe, a greater amount of good intention has been lost, than by the direct assault of enemies apparently more powerful.

Again, the indolence almost necessarily induced by the enjoyment to a great extent of the luxuries of life—how often is this foe to health and cheerfulness dressed up in the cloak of charity, and made to assume the character of kindness to the poor, in offering them employment. Not that I would be guilty of endeavoring to divert from so necessitous a channel the proper exercise of *real* charity; but at the same time that we advocate the cause of the poor, let us call things by their right names; and if we employ more servants than are necessary, or send out our work to be done by those who need the utmost amount of what we give them for doing it, let us not take advantage of this disposition of our affairs, to spend the time which remains upon our hands in idleness; but let us rather employ, in a higher sphere of usefulness, those faculties of mind, and those advantages of education, the free exercise of which constitutes one of the greatest privileges of an exalted station.

The same temptations which spread the snare of indolence around the feet of the unwary, are equally potent in their power to beguile into habits of self-indulgence. And here the fancied or real delicacy of constitution which seems in the present day to be the birthright of Englishwomen, with all that spectral host of nervous maladies, which so often paralyze their energies, and render nugatory their efforts to do good—here, in this most privileged of all positions of human life, most frequently assail the female frame, so as often to reduce their pitiable victim to a mere nonentity as regards one great end of her existence—usefulness to her fellow-creatures.

Far be it from me to speak with unkindness or want of sympathy of those maladies of mind and body, which, under the general head of nervous disorders, I believe to constitute some of the greatest miseries which "flesh is heir to." But having never found them to exist to any serious extent where constant occupation of head and hand, and heathful bodily exercise, were kept up with vigorous and unremitting effort; I feel the more anxious that English wives should not create for themselves, out of their habits of personal indulgence, so formidable an enemy to their own enjoyment, and to the beneficial influence which, as Christian women, they are capable of exercising to an almost incalculable extent.

I feel anxious also, that some pictures, too frequently witnessed by us all, should never be realized in their experience—pictures in which a sickly, helpless, desponding wife, forms the centre of a group of neglected children, whose boisterous mirth she is little able to endure, and whose numerous wants, all unrestrained, remind her every moment, with fresh pain, of her inability to gratify them.

That a woman thus situated, is, under existing circumstances, more to be pitied than blamed, we should be wanting in common feeling to deny ; but in comparing her situation with that of a healthy, active, cheerful-spirited wife, prompt to answer every claim, and happy in the discharge of every duty ; and when we see how such a woman, merely by the exercise of moral power, and often without the advantages of any extraordinary intellectual gifts, can become the living principle of activity, order, and cheerfulness in her own family, the adviser whom all consult, the comforter to whom all repair, and the support upon whom all depend, happy in herself, and diffusing happiness around her —oh how we long that those dispositions, and those habits, both of mind and body, should be cultivated in early youth, which would be most likely to ensure such blessed results as the experience of riper years !

Much of this habitual cheerfulness, and this willing submission to the requirements of duty, is to be attained by the proper regulation of our aims with regard to common things ; but especially by having chosen a right standard of excellence for every thing we do. For want of aiming at the right thing, the whole course of human life, which might be so richly diversified with enjoyment of various kinds, is often converted into a long, fruitless, and wearisome struggle, first to attain a happiness which is never found, and then to escape a misery which too surely pursues its mistaken victim.

The married woman cannot, then, too frequently ask herself, " What is it which constitutes the object of my greatest earthly desire ? and at what standard do I really aim ?" Nor let us deceive ourselves either in asking or in answering these questions ; for if it be essential to integrity that we should be sincere with others, it is no less so that we should be sincere with ourselves.

If, then, we are weak enough to aim at being the centre of a brilliant circle, let us not pretend that we court notoriety for the purpose of extending our influence, and through that, our means of doing good. If we aim at surpassing our neighbors in the richness of of our furniture, the splendor of our entertainments, and the costliness of our dress, let us not deceive ourselves into the belief, that it is for the sake of encouraging the manufactures and the people of our own country. If we aim at taking the lead in affairs of moment, and occupying the first place among those with whom we associate, let us not do this under the plea of being forced into a conspicuous situation against our will, in compliance with the wish of others, and under the fear of giving them offence. Let us, I repeat, be honest with ourselves, for this is our only chance of ever arriving at any satisfactory conclusion, or attaining any desirable end.

And if we would ascertain with certainty what is the actual standard of excellence which in idea we set up for ourselves, for all persons, whether they know it or not, have such a standard, we have only to ascertain to what particular purpose our thoughts and actions most uniformly tend. If the most brilliant and striking characters are those which we consider most enviable, we may easily detect in ourselves a prevailing endeavor, in what we say or do, to produce an impression, and consequently to render ourselves conspicuous, than which, nothing can be more out of keeping with the right position of a married woman, nor more likely to render her, at the summit of her wishes, a mark for envy, and all uncharitableness.

But a far more frequent, and more extensively prevailing standard of excellence, is that which consists in giving the best dinners, exhibiting the most costly furniture, being dressed in the newest fashion, and making every entertainment go off in the most successful manner. How many heads and hearts are made to ache by this ambition, it must be left for the private history of every family to record. What sleepless nights, what days of toil, what torturing anxieties, what envyings, what disputes, what backbitings, and what bitter disappointments arise out of this very cause, must be left for the same record to disclose. And if in the opposite scale we would weigh the happiness enjoyed, the good imparted, or the evil overcome by the operation of the same agency, we behold a blank; for let the measure of success be what it may, there is no extreme of excellence to which this ambition leads, but it may be exceeded by a neighbor, or perhaps a friend; and where wealth can purchase all that we aspire to, we must ever be liable to the mortifying chance of being compelled to yield precedence to the ignorant and the vulgar-minded.

Nothing, in fact, can be more vulgar, or more in accordance with the lowest grade of feeling, than an ambition of this kind. Not only is it low in its own nature, but low in all the calculations it requires, in all the faculties it calls into exercise, and in all the associations it draws along with it. Yet, who shall dethrone this monster from its place in the hearts of English wives, where it gives the law to private conduct, levies a tax upon industry, monopolizes pecuniary profit, makes itself the arbiter in cases of difficulty or doubt, rules the destiny of families, and finally gives the tone to public feeling, and consequently the bias to national character?

I ask again, who shall dethrone this monster? Perhaps there would be little weight attached to my assertion, if I were to say that it is within the sphere of woman's influence to do this; that it rests with the wives of England to choose whether they will go on to estimate their position in society by the cost of their furniture, and the brilliance of their entertainments; or, by the moral and intellectual character of their social intercourse, by the high principle which regulates their actions, and by the domestic happiness to be found within their homes.

So long as we esteem those we meet with in society according to the fashion of their dress, the richness of their ornaments, or the style in which they live, it is a mockery of words to say that our standard of excellence does not consist in that which money can purchase, or a vain and vulgar ambition attain. And so long as we feel cast down, disappointed, and distressed at being outshone in these outward embellishments, it is a certain proof that we are not attaching supreme importance to such as adorn the mind.

I am fully aware, in writing on this subject, that I am but lifting a feeble voice against the giant-force of popular feeling; that the state of our country, presenting an almost universal tendency towards an excess of civilization, added to the improvement in our manufactures, and the facility with which every kind of luxury is now obtained, are causes perpetually operating upon the great mass of the people, so as to urge them on to a state of eager competition in the display of all which money can procure; and that this competition is highly applauded by many, as beneficial to the nation at large, and especially so when that nation is considered merely as a mass of instrumentality, operating upon what is purely material.

But I am aware also, that this very cause, operating so widely and so powerfully as it does, ought to furnish the impetus of a new movement in society, by which the intellectual and the spiritual shall, by a fresh effort, be roused to its proper elevation above the material; and this necessary and truly noble effort, I must again repeat, it is in the power of the wives of England to make.

Nor would this great movement in reality be so difficult to effect, as we might be led to suppose from looking only at the surface of society, and observing the multiplicity of instances in which a false standard of excellence is established. We are sometimes too much influenced in our opinions, as well as too much discouraged in our endeavors to do good, by a superficial observation of the general state of things in social life; for there is often an under-current of feeling towards what is just and good, at work in the minds of those who, from being deficient in the moral power to act upon their own convictions, fall in with the superficial tide, and go along with the stream, against their better judgment, if not against their real inclinations.

Thus, in a more close and intimate acquaintance with the world, we find, to our frequent satisfaction, that a combination of intellectual superiority and moral worth, is not in reality so lightly esteemed as at first we had supposed; that the weak and the vain, who spend their lives in striving after that which truly profiteth not, are dissatisfied and weary with their own fruitless efforts, and that others a little more gifted with understanding, and enlightened by juster views, though engaged in the same unprofitable struggle, would be more than glad of any thing that would assist them to escape from their grovelling anxieties, and low entanglements, so as in an open and decided manner to declare themselves on the side of what is intrinsically good, and consequently worthy of their utmost endeavors to attain.

Thus we find too, in spite of popular prejudice against a simple dress, or a homely way of living, that respectability, and genuine worth of character, are able not only to give dignity to any position in society, but also to command universal respect from others; and that, while few are bold enough to imitate, there is no small proportion of the community who secretly wish they were like those noble-minded individuals, who dare to aim at a true standard of excellence in the formation of their own habits, and the general conduct of their families.

Shall we then go on in the same way, forcing ourselves to be contemptible, and despising the bondage to which we submit? It is true, the effort necessary to be made, which the state of the times, and the satisfaction of our consciences, alike require of us, is hard for any single individual. But let us stand by each other in this great and noble cause. Let the strong endeavor to encourage and sustain the weak; and let us prove, for the benefit of succeeding generations, how much may be done for the happiness of our homes, and the good of our country, by being satis-

fied with the position in which Providence has placed us, and by endeavoring to adorn that position with the lasting embellishments which belong to an enlightened understanding, a well-regulated mind, and a benevolent, sincere, and faithful heart.

Our standard of excellence will then be no longer found in the most splendid jewelry, or the costliest plate; for in all these the vulgar and the ignorant may easily attain pre-eminence; but in the warmest welcome, the kindest service, the best-regulated household, the strictest judgment of ourselves, the most beneficial influence, the highest hopes for futurity, and the largest amount of domestic and social happiness which it is ever permitted to the families of earth to enjoy.

It is needless to say that all these embellishments to life may be ensured without regard to position in society; and if such were made the universal standard of excellence among the wives of England, much, if not all, the suffering which prevails wherever happiness is made to consist in what money can procure, would cease to be found within our homes; while, rising thus above our circumstances, we should no longer be subject in our hopes and fears to the fluctuations of commerce, or the uncertainty of a position depending solely upon its pecuniary advantages. We should then feel to be resting on a sure foundation, just in proportion as our standard was faithfully upheld. I do not say that we should be free from troubles, for such are the lot of all; but that single wide-spreading source of anxiety, which from its vastness appears in the present day to swallow up all others—the anxiety to attain a position higher than our own proper sphere, would then vanish from our land; and with it such a host of grievances, that in contemplating so blessed a change in our domestic and social condition, I cannot but again entreat the wives of England to think of these things, and finally to unite together in one firm determination to establish a new and a better standard by which to estimate their position in society.

CHAPTER IX.

DOMESTIC MANAGEMENT.

CLOSELY connected with the subject already dwelt upon, is that of domestic management; since whatever standard we choose, and whatever principles we adopt as our rule of action, will develop themselves in the system we pursue with regard to the conduct of our domestic affairs.

If, therefore, to appear well with the world according to the popular standard, be our supreme desire, the tendency of our domestic regulations will be to make, before our friends and associates, the greatest possible display of what is costly and elegant in our furniture and style of living; while, on the other hand, if our aim be to ensure the greatest amount of happiness to ourselves, and to those around us, we shall have a widely different task to pursue; and it is to the latter purpose only that I propose devoting this chapter, as the former could be better effected by consulting the upholsterer, the silversmith, or the jeweller.

Leaving to individuals thus qualified the important office of deciding what is according to the latest fashion, and which article is most approved in circles of distinction, we must turn our attention to a study of a totally different description; and if at first it should appear more difficult and complicated, it will have the merit of becoming every day more simple, and more clear; or if it should seem to involve by necessity a certain degree of suffering and self-denial, it will have the still higher merit of resulting in ultimate happiness; while the system of domestic management above alluded to, though in the outset full of promises of indulgence and pleasure, is certain to involve in greater and deeper perplexity the longer it is pursued, and finally to issue in vexation and. disappointment.

It is, then, the way to make others happy, and consequently to be happy ourselves, which I am about to recommend; and if in doing this I am compelled to enter into the minute and homely details of woman's daily life, I must claim the forbearance of the reader on the plea that no act can be so trifling as not to be ennobled by a great or a generous motive.

Before proceeding further with this subject, I must address one word to the ladies of the present day—to the refined and fastidious, who dwell in an atmosphere of taste, and make that their standard of excellence—lest from the freedom of my remarks upon dress and furniture, I should fall under their condemnation for undervaluing what is elegant, and wishing to discard what is ornamental; or, in other words, of being indifferent to the influence of beauty in general, as it may justly be said to refine our feelings, and enhance our enjoyments.

Without presuming to refer such readers to a work of my own,* in which they would find that my admiration of the beautiful, wherever it may be found, is scarcely inferior to theirs; I will simply express my conviction, that the exercise of good taste, which must ever be in accordance with the principles of beauty, fitness, and harmony, is by no means confined to the display of what is costly, elaborate, or superb; but may at all times be sufficiently developed in the arrangement of what is simple and appropriate. Indeed, there are nicer distinctions, and more exquisite sensibilities, required in the happy distribution of limited means, than in the choice and arrangement of the most costly ornaments which money can procure. In accordance with this fact, we almost invariably find writers of fiction bestowing what is gorgeous and elaborate upon scenes and characters with which the best feelings of the heart have little connection; while the favorite heroine is universally made conspicuous in her simplicity, and at the same time pre-eminent in her good taste.

But in addition to other considerations, it is in the present day so easy as to be common, and consequently to some extent vulgar, for all persons, both high and low, to adorn themselves and their houses to the

---

* The Poetry of Life.

extent of their pecuniary means;
ey are also enabled to do this with
tin appearance of taste, because to
tss of persons who supply the requi-
:icles of dress and furniture, it has
: their study to ascertain what is most
ed in the highest circles, as well as
s most ornamental and becoming in
And thus individuals who have but
tste themselves, may easily supply
:ficiency by consulting what are called
:t tradespeople, or those who sell to
hest purchasers.

much more exquisite, then, must be
od taste, and delicate feeling, of her
ts no such assistance to call in; who
s but little money upon the entertain-
f her friends, in order that she may
m the oftener, and with a less painful
on her household; but who is still able
onduct her household arrangements,
hile there is no distressing appearance
essive preparation to alarm her guests,
ect of elegance and comfort is thrown
te most familiar things, so as to convey
:a of her family affairs being always
ted in strict accordance with the prin-
of taste—of that taste which consults
tuty of fitness and order, and which
s no extravagance or excess to inter-
th the perfect harmony of its arrange-

t, then, we see the value of having
rood taste one of the studies of early
'r when the cares and anxieties of a
told, added to the actual occupations
mistress of a family, press upon the
mes over-burdened wife, she will find
me, and perhaps less inclination, to en-
) any abstruse calculations upon these
; and hence we too frequently see
married women, a deterioration of
ter in this respect; for where one
woman is careless and slovenly in her
ance or habits, there is reason to fear
ght find many in the married state,
tight justly be suspected of having lost
agard for those embellishments which
l upon the exercise of good taste.

In pursuing the subject of domestic management, we are again struck with the importance of speaking of things by their proper
names; for by some strange misnomer, those
women have come to be generally called good
managers, who put their whole souls into the
business of providing for the mere bodily ex-
igences of every day; and thus the more refined, and sometimes the more intellectual,
who have no idea how many good principles
may be exemplified in the proper regulation
of a household, have imbibed a sort of distaste for good management, as if it necessarily belonged exclusively to the province of
the ignorant, or the vulgar-minded.

Managers, indeed, those household tor-
ments may be, who live perpetually in an
element of strife and discord, where no one
who valued their own peace would wish to
live with them; but *good* managers they certainly are not. It is not, therefore, in absolute bustle and activity, nor yet in mere cleanliness, order, and punctuality, that the perfection of domestic management consists; for
where the members of a household are made
to feel that they pay too dearly, by the loss
of their peace and comfort, for the cleanliness, order, and punctuality of the mistress,
all claim on her part to the merit of *good*
management must be relinquished.

It is most difficult, however, to be sufficiently solicitous about such points of observance, and not irritated by the neglect of them
in others. Hence it is often said that ill-
tempered servants are the cleanest and most
orderly; because the exactness and precision
which regulate their conduct, produce in unenlightened minds, a tendency to exact the
same from others; and where this is impossible to be effected, produce a petulance and
dissatisfaction which obtain for them the character of being ill-tempered; while an opposite
disposition, careless of order, cleanliness, or
punctuality, obtains sometimes with great injustice the merit of being good-tempered,
simply because any deviation from these
points occasions to such a mind no disturbance whatever.

It has appeared to me ever since I was capable of extreme annoyance or extreme enjoyment from such causes, that the perfection of good domestic management required so many excellences both of head and heart, as to render it a study well worth the attention of the most benevolent and enlightened of human beings. For when we consider the simple fact, that it comprehends—nay, is mainly dependent upon the art of giving to every thing which comes within the sphere of practical duty its proper weight, and consequently its due share of relative importance, we see at once that it cannot be within the province of a common or a vulgar mind consistently to do this, more especially as there must not only be the perception to find out, and the judgment to decide upon things generally, but the good feeling—and here is the great point—to make that subservient which is properly inferior. Thus all selfish considerations must be set aside, all low calculations, all caprice, all vanity, all spite. And in how many instances do all these, with a multitude of other enemies to peace and happiness, mix themselves up with what people persist in calling *good* management, but which from this lamentable admixture, makes nobody like such management, or wish to be where it prevails!

Perhaps it has occurred to not a few of us to see one of these reputed good managers, bustling about a house from one apartment to another, peeping into corners, throwing open closets, emptying drawers, with a countenance which bid defiance for the time to every gentle or kindly feeling; and calling to one person, despatching another, or enumerating the misdeeds of a third, with a voice which even in its distant and unintelligible utterance, had the bitter tone of raking up old grievances, and throwing them about like firebrands on every side. And then the bursting forth of the actual eruption, where such a volcano was perpetually at work! The fusion of heated and heterogeneous particles into one general mass—the outpouring indiscriminate and vast—the flame, the smoke, the tumult! what is there, I would ask, in the absence of harmless dust, or in the presence

of the richest and best concocted food, to repay the wretched family where such a manager presides, for what must be endured through the course of any single day?

No—let me live in peace, is the natural demand of every human heart; and so far as relates to our cookery, and our carpets, we are happily all able to do this. We must, therefore, settle it in our minds, that whatever excellences may be attained in the preparation of food, the care of clothing, the arrangement of furniture, or the general order of rooms, that can never be called good management, which fails to secure peace, and to promote happiness.

Not that I would undervalue the care of the body, so far as tends to preserve health, and ensure cheerfulness; or, what is still more important, so far as serves to evince a high degree of tenderness and affection, strong evidence of which may sometimes be conveyed through this channel, when no other is open. It is the *supreme* importance attached to these cares and anxieties, which prevents such a system of management being properly called good.

In order to maintain general cheerfulness, and promote happiness throughout your household, it is essential that you cultivate within your own mind, a feeling of contentment with your home, your servants, and your domestic affairs in general, remembering that nothing which occurs to you in this department is the result of mere chance, but that all your trials, as well as your enjoyments, are appointed by a kind Providence, who knows better than you can know, exactly what is ultimately best for you. It is consequently no more a deviation from what you ought to be prepared to expect, that your servants should sometimes do wrong, that your plans should be thwarted by folly and perverseness, or that your house should be old and inconvenient; than that the blossoms in your garden should occasionally be blighted, or that a shower should fall at the moment you had fixed for going out.

Yet, to maintain this desirable cheerfulness through all circumstances, is certainly no easy task, unless both health and temper have been carefully attended to before marriage; for when the former fails, it is but natural that the animal spirits should fail too; and defects of temper if long indulged, so as to have grown into habit, will, in the general conduct of domestic affairs, be able to infuse a taint of bitterness into the kindest endeavors, so as effectually to defeat the best intentions.

How necessary is it, therefore, for all women to have learned to manage themselves, before undertaking the management of a household, for the charge is both a serious, and a comprehensive one; and however inexperienced a wife may be, however helpless, uncalculating, and unequal to the task, she no sooner takes upon herself the duties of a mistress, than she becomes, in a great measure, responsible for the welfare of every member of the family over which she presides. And not only is this her situation in the ordinary course of things, but on all extraordinary occasions, she must be at the same post, ever on the alert, prompt to direct, and ready with expedients suited to every emergency that may occur.

In cases of illness more especially, though the more laborious duties of the sick-room may with propriety be deputed to others, there can be no excuse for the mistress who does not make it her business to see that proper attention is paid to the directions of the doctor, as well as to the ventilation of rooms, and all those other means of alleviating pain, or facilitating recovery, instead of which, inexperienced nurses are so apt to substitute notions and nostrums of their own.

But beyond the care of the patient, that of the nurse also devolves upon the mistress of the house, to see that her wants are properly supplied, that a judicious distribution of her time is made, so as to allow of a reasonable portion of rest; or, if wearied out, to take care that her place is supplied, so that none may have to complain of hardship or oppression. And here we may observe by the way, that this kind of care and consideration bestowed upon those who habitually bear the burden of domestic labor, constitutes one of the strongest bonds which can exist between a mistress and her servants; besides rewarding her, in many instances, by a double measure of their gratitude and their faithfulness.

If the mistress of the house, as is not unfrequently the case with kind-hearted women, should take charge of the patient herself, it then becomes her duty not to act so entirely from the impulse of feeling, as to neglect her own health. I mention this, because there is a kind of romantic devotion to the duties of the sick-room, more especially where the sufferer is an object of interest or affection, which carries on the young nurse from one day of solicitude to another, without refreshment, without rest, and without exercise in the open air, until nature being completely exhausted, she herself becomes a source of trouble, and an object of anxiety and care. By this apparent generosity, the kindest intentions are often frustrated; while the household of such a mistress will necessarily be thrown into alarm and disorder, at the very time when it is most important that order and quiet should be maintained throughout.

To those who please themselves with the idea that such romantic self-devotion is the extreme of generosity, it may appear a cold kind of reasoning to advocate the importance of self-preservation, by frequently taking exercise at short intervals in the open air. Yet, I own I am one of those who prefer the kindness which lasts, to that which expends itself in sudden and violent effort; and I would, therefore, strongly urge upon the wife not only to attend to such means of prolonging her own usefulness, but to see that the nurse employed under her direction does the same.

Nor is it only in such cases as that already described, that married women are apt to neglect the best means of maintaining cheerfulness, and preserving health, two blessings which they above all other persons have the most reason to estimate highly. Not that I would insinuate an idea of any culpable neglect of the employment of doctors, or the use of medicines. I believe this can scarcely be charged upon the wives of England, as a general fault. But I have known some women almost entirely neglect all kinds of exercise in the open air, either because they were too busy, or it tired them too much; or, for that most amiable of all reasons, because their husbands were absent, and they were too dependent to walk alone. And thus, from the very excess of their affection, they were satisfied, on a husband's return, to be weary, listless, dispirited, and altogether incapable of adding to his enjoyment, whatever he—happy man that he must be, to be so tenderly beloved!—might add to theirs.

But fortunately for the character of woman, and may we not add, for the patience of man, there are happier methods of proving the existence of affection than that which is exhibited by the display either of an excessive and imprudent self-devotion, which effectually defeats its own object; or a weak and childish dependence, which is nothing better than a sort of disguised selfishness. In accordance with deeper and more chastened feelings of regard, is that system of careful but quiet watchfulness over the general health of a husband, or a family, which detects every symptom of indisposition, and provides against all unnecessary aggravation of such symptoms by any arrangement of domestic affairs which can be made so as to spare an invalid, or prevent the occurrence of illness.

I believe that nothing tends more to the increase of those diseases classed in popular phraseology under the head of bilious, which prevail so extensively in the present day, than long fasting, with heavy meals at the close of the day. Where fashion is the root of this evil, it is to be supposed that the sufferers have their own reward; at all events, a mere matter of choice, it would be impertinence to interfere with; but in the case of those husbands whose business calls them from home during the greater part of every day, surely something might be done by the wife, to break through this habit, either by supplying them with intermediate refreshment, or inducing them by persuasion or argument to make some different distribution of their time.

And where symptoms of indisposition do appear, how beautiful is that display of affection in a wife, who can put aside all her own little ailments for the more important consideration of those of a husband; who can bear without a murmur to have her domestic affairs at any moment deranged, so as may best suit his feelings or his health; and who can make up her mind with promptness and cheerfulness, even to accompany him from home, at any sacrifice of her own comfort and convenience! How precious then is the health and the ability to do this, and to do it with energy, and perfect good-will—how much more precious than the childish fondness to which allusion has already been made, which would lead her to sit and faint beside him in his illness, or to neglect the exercise necessary for her own health, because, forsooth, she could not walk without him!

Nor let it be imagined from the familiar and apparently trifling nature of the instances adduced in relation to the subject of domestic management, that the subject itself is one of little moment. Necessity compels the selection of only a few cases from the mass of evidence which might be brought to prove how many important principles may be acted upon in the familiar transactions of every day. The woman of naturally restless and irritable temper, for instance, who, without controlling her own feelings, would effectually destroy the peace of every member of her household, may by habits of self-government, and by a kind and disinterested regard for the happiness of those around her, so far restrain the natural impetuosity of her character, as to become a blessing instead of a torment to the household over which she presides; while the tender and affectionate wife, who would fondly and foolishly waste her strength by incessant watching over a husband, or a child, may, by the habit of making impulse subservient to judgment, preserve her health for the service of many a future day, and thus render herself, what every married woman ought to be—the support and the comfort of her whole household.

We see here, although the instances themselves may appear insignificant, that in these two cases are exemplified the great principles of disinterested kindness, prudence, and self-government. And thus it is with every act that falls within the sphere of female duty. The act itself may be trifling; but the motives by which it is sustained may be such as to do honor to the religion we profess. And we must ever bear in mind, that not only do we honor that religion by engaging in public services on behalf of our fellow-creatures, or for the good of our own souls; but by restraining evil tempers, and selfish dispositions, in the privacy of our own domestic sphere; and by cherishing for purposes of practical usefulness, those amiable and benevolent feelings, which are not only most endearing to our fellow-creatures, but most in accordance with the perfection of the Christian character.

In turning our attention again to the practical part of female duty, as connected with domestic management, that important study which refers to the best means of economizing time and money, is forcibly presented to our notice. Having dwelt at considerable length upon the subject of economy of time in a former work,* I shall not repeat the arguments there made use of to show the importance of this great principle of good management; but simply state, that if essential before marriage to the attainment of intellectual or moral good, and to the welfare and comfort of those with whom we are connected; it becomes doubly so when the mistress of a house has not only to economize her own time, but to portion out that of others.

In this, as in all other cases where good influence is made the foundation of rightly-exercised authority, the married woman must not forget that example goes before precept. Whatever then may be the trial to her natural feelings, she will, if actuated by this principle, begin the day by rising early; for it is in vain to urge others to do what they see that we have not either the strength, or not the inclination to do ourselves. Besides which, there is little inducement for servants or other inferior members of a family to rise early, when they know that the business of the day will be delayed by the mistress herself not being ready; while, on the other hand, if prepared to expect that she will be up early herself, there are few who could be so unaccommodating as to thwart her wishes by not endeavoring to be ready at the appointed time.

Nor is there any thing depending upon ourselves which tends more to the proper regulation of the mind, as well as the household, than the habit of rising early—so early as to have time to think, as most persons do in the morning hours, clearly and dispassionately; when, free from the disturbance of feeling so often excited by contact with others, the mind is at liberty to draw its own conclusions, from a general survey of the actual state of things, uninterrupted by any partial impressions received through the medium of the outward senses. Thus it often happens, that in the early morning we are brought to serious and just conclusions, which we should never have arrived at, where the actual circumstances which gave rise to our reflections, were transpiring beneath our notice, or had the persons most intimately connected with such circumstances been present during the formation of our opinions.

The morning, then, is the time for reviewing the actions and events of the previous day, and for forming, for that which has commenced, a new set of plans, upon the convictions which such a calm and impartial review is calculated to produce. The morning is the time for gathering our thoughts together, for arranging our resources, and for asking with humble reverence that Divine assistance, without which we have no right to expect that the coming day will be spent more satisfactorily than the past.

Such are the higher advantages derived from habits of early rising, but there are also practical duties to be attended to by all mar-

---

* The Daughters of England.

ried women, in the commencement of the day, which must be so managed as not to interfere with, or delay the business of others; or the end of early rising will be entirely defeated, as regards its good influence upon the general habits of a family.

I mention this, because there are some well-intentioned persons, who habitually rise early, and are yet habitually too late for breakfast, wondering not the less every day how it can possibly be that they are so. To such I would venture to hint, that *despatch* is an excellent thing in whatever we have to do; and that the habit of trifling is one of the most formidable enemies to good intention in this respect, because at the same time that it hinders our practical usefulness, it beguiles us into the belief, that we are actually doing something—nay, even a great deal; yet, look to the end, and nothing is really done.

If such persons are unacquainted with the merits of despatch, or refuse to adopt it as a wiser and a better rule, I know of nothing they can do, except it be to rise a little earlier, and a little earlier still, until they find that they have exactly proportioned their time to their requirements; but on no account ought they to allow the breakfast, or the business of the day, to be retarded so as to meet their convenience. Whatever time they take from sleep is their own, and they have a right to dispose of it as they please; but that time can scarcely be called so, which is portioned out to others, especially where it is barely sufficient for the business they are required to do through the course of the day.

Perhaps it is with us all too frequent a mistake to suppose that time is our own, and that the higher our station, and consequently the greater the number of persons subject to our control, the more entirely this is the case. I have already said that the time we take from sleep, may with some justice be called so; but except in a state of existence entirely isolated, and exempt from relative duties, I am not aware how conscientious persons can trifle with time, and not feel that they are encroaching upon the rights of others, to say nothing of the more serious responsibility

neglected by the waste of so valuable a talent committed to their trust.

There is no time perhaps so entirely wasted as that which is spent in waiting for others, because while expectation is kept up that each moment will terminate our suspense, we cannot prudently engage in any other occupation. If, then, the mistress of a house, by habitual delay of breakfast, keeps as many as four persons waiting half an hour every morning, she is the cause of two valuable hours being wasted to them, which they would most probably have preferred spending in any other way rather than in waiting for her.

It must of course be allowed, that every master and mistress of a family enjoys the right of breakfasting as late as they choose, provided they give directions accordingly; but where there is one in the middle ranks of society who will order breakfast at ten, there are twenty who will order it at eight, and not be ready before nine. It can only be to such deviations from arrangements made by the heads of the family, and understood by all its members, that the foregoing observations apply.

It is a great point in the economy of time, that different kinds of work should be made to fill up different intervals. Hence the great value of having a variety of needlework, knitting, &c.; for besides the astonishing amount which may thus almost imperceptibly be done, a spirit of contentment and cheerfulness is much promoted by having the hands constantly employed. Thus, if ever the mistress of a house spends what is called the dark hours in idleness, it is a proof that she has either not properly studied the arts of knitting and netting; or that she is a very indifferent workwoman not to be able to pay for the use of candles. Could such persons once be brought to appreciate the really beneficial effects of constant employment upon the mind and temper, could they taste those sweet musings, or enjoy those ingatherings of thought, which are carried on while a piece of work is growing beneath their hands, they would never again require urging to those habits of industry which may truly be said to bring with them their own reward.

Habitually idle persons are apt to judge of the difficulty of being industrious, by what it costs them to do any thing they may happen to undertake; the movements of a naturally indolent person being composed of a series of painful exertions, while the activity of an industrious person resembles the motion of a well-regulated machine, which, having been once set at work, requires comparatively little force to keep it going. It is consequently by making industry a habit, and by no other means, that it can be thoroughly enjoyed; for if between one occupation and another, time is allowed for sensations of weariness to be indulged, or for doubts to be entertained as to what shall be done next, with those who have much to do all such endeavors to be industrious must necessarily be irksome, if not absolutely laborious.

How pitiable then is the situation of that married woman who has never fully realized the true enjoyment of industry, nor the advantages of passing rapidly from one occupation to another, as if it was the business of life to keep doing, rather than to wait to see what was to be done, and to question the necessity of doing it! Pitiable, indeed, is that woman, because in a well-regulated household, even where the mistress takes no part in the executive business herself, there must still be a constant oversight, and constant forethought, accompanied with a variety of calculations, plans, and arrangements, which to an indolent person cannot fail to be irksome in the extreme; while to one who has been accustomed to rely upon her own resources in the constant exercise of industry, they give a zest and an interest to all the duties of life, and at the same time impart a feeling of contentment and cheerfulness sufficient of itself to render every duty light.

There is no case in which example is more closely connected with influence than in this. A company of idle persons can keep each other in countenance to almost any extent; while there are few who cannot be made ashamed of idleness by having constantly before them an example of industry. Thus where the mistress of a house on extraordinary occasions is ever ready to lend assistance herself; where she evinces a decided preference for doing things with her own hand, rather than seeing them left undone; and where it is known that her mind is as quick to perceive what is wanted as her hand is willing to execute it; such a mistress will seldom have to complain that her servants are idle, or that they cannot be brought to make the necessary effort when extra work has to be done.

There is, however, a just medium to be observed between doing too much, and too little, in domestic affairs; and this point of observance must be regulated entirely by the circumstances of the family, and the number of servants employed. It can never be said that the atmosphere of the kitchen is an element in which a refined and intellectual woman ought to live; though the department itself is one which no sensible woman would think it a degradation to overlook. But instead of maintaining a general oversight and arrangement of such affairs, some well-intentioned women plunge head, heart, and hand into the vortex of culinary operations, thinking, feeling, and doing what would be more appropriately left to their servants.

This fault, however, is one which belongs but little to the present times. It was the fault of our grandmothers, and we are endeavoring to improve upon their habits by falling into the opposite extreme, forgetting, in our eagerness to secure to ourselves personal ease and indulgence, how many good and kind feelings may be brought into exercise by a participation in the practical part of domestic management—how much valuable health, and how much vivacity and cheerfulness, alternating with wholesome and real rest, are purchased by habits of personal activity.

But it is impossible to do justice to this subject without entering into it fully, and at considerable length; and having already done this elsewhere,* under the head of "Kindness and Consideration," I will spare the reader a repetition of my own sentiments upon a subject of such vital importance to the wives of England.

CHAPTER X.

ORDER, JUSTICE, AND BENEVOLENCE.

THE general tendency of domestic management should be, to establish throughout a household the principles of order, justice, and benevolence.

In speaking first of order, I would not be understood to restrict the meaning of the word to such points of observance as the placing of chairs in a drawing-room, or ornaments on a mantelpiece. The principle of order, in its happiest development, has to do with the state of the mind, as well as the personal habits. Thus a due regard to the general fitness of things, correct calculations as to time and means, with a just sense of relative importance, so as to keep the less subservient to the greater, all belong to the department of order in a well-governed household, and should all be exemplified in the general conduct of the mistress.

There is no surer method of maintaining authority over others, than by showing that we have learned to govern ourselves. Thus a well-ordered mind obtains an influence in society, which it would be impossible for mere talent, without this regard to order, ever to acquire. All caprice, all hasty or violent expressions, all sudden and extravagant ebullitions of feeling of any kind whatever, exhibited before servants and inferiors, have a tendency to lower the dignity of a mistress, and consequently to weaken her influence.

The mistress of a house should always appear calm, and perfectly self-possessed,

whether she feels so or not; and if from an accumulation of household disasters, particularly such as mal-occurrences before her guests, the agitation of her feelings should be too great for her powers of self-control, she may always find a natural and appropriate outlet for them, by sympathizing with other sufferers in the same calamity, and thus evincing her regard for them, rather than for herself.

Nor ought we to class this species of self-discipline with those artificial manners which are assumed merely for the sake of effect. If the same individual who controlled her feelings before her guests, should go out among her servants and give full vent to them there, such a case would certainly deserve to be so classed. But the self-control I would gladly recommend, is of a widely different order, extending to a mastery over the feelings, as well as the expressions. In the former case, a lady seated at the head of her table, will sometimes speak in a sharp whisper to a servant, with a countenance in which all the furies might be represented as one; when suddenly turning to her guests, she will address them with the blandest smiles, even before the cloud has had time to vanish from her brow. In the latter case, the mistress of the house will recollect, that others have been made to suffer perhaps more than herself, and that whatever the cause of vexation or distress may be, it can only be making that distress greater, for her to appear angry or disturbed. By such habits of reflection, and by the mastery of judgment over impulse, she will be able in time, not only to appear calm, but really to feel so; or if there should be just as much excitement as may be agreeably carried off in condolence with her friends, there will never be sufficient really to destroy either their comfort, or her own peace of mind.

In speaking of the beauty of order, would that it were possible to impress this fact upon the minds of English wives—that there is neither beauty nor order in making their servants and their domestic affairs in general the subject of conversation in company. To

---

* The Women of England.

hear some good ladies talking, one would really think that servants were a sort of plague sent upon the nation at large, and upon them in particular. To say nothing of the wrong state of feeling evinced by allowing one of our greatest sources of personal comfort to be habitually regarded as a bane rather than a blessing; we see here one of those instances in which the laws of order are infringed by a disregard to the fitness of things; for however interesting our domestic affairs may be to ourselves, it requires but little tact or observation to discover, that they interest no one else, unless it be our nearest and most intimate friends, whose personal regard to us will induce them to listen with kindness to whatever we describe as being connected with our welfare or happiness.

Upon the same principle, a history of bodily ailments should never be forced upon visitors; for as it requires either to be an intimate friend, or a member of the same family, to feel any particular interest in the good or bad practices of servants; so it requires that our friends should be very tenderly attached to us to care about our ailments, or even to listen with any real attention when we make them the subject of conversation. In all such cases, it is possible that a third party may be more quick to perceive the real state of things than the party most concerned; but I own I have often wondered what the habitual complainer of household and personal grievances could find to induce her to go on in the averted look, the indifferent answer, and the absent manner of her guests; yet, such is the entire occupation of some minds with subjects of this nature, that they are scarcely alive to impressions from any other source; and perhaps the surest way to prevent our annoyance of others, is to recollect how often and how much we have been annoyed in this way ourselves.

It is, then, no mean or trifling attainment for the mistress of a house to be thoroughly at home in her own domestic affairs; deeply interested in the character and habits of all the different members of her household, so as to extend over them the care and the solici-

tude of a mother; and yet before her guests, or in the presence of her friends, to be perfectly disengaged, able to enter into all their causes of anxiety, or hope, and above all, to give an intellectual character and a moral tendency to the general tone of the conversation in which she takes a part. With nothing less than this strict regulation of the feelings, as well as the habits, this regard to fitness, and this maintenance of order in the subserviency of one thing to another, ought the wives of England to be satisfied; for it is to them we look for every important bias given to the manners and the morals of that class of society upon which depends so much of the good influence of England as a nation.

A love of order is as much exemplified by doing any thing at its proper time as in its appropriate place; and it rests with a mistress of a house to see that her own time, and that of her servants, is judiciously proportioned out. Some mistresses, forgetting this, and unacquainted with the real advantages of order, are in the habit of calling their servants from one occupation to another, choosing extra work for them to do on busy days, crowding a variety of occupations into one short space of time, and then complaining that nothing is thoroughly done; while others will put off necessary preparations until so late that everybody is flurried and confused, and well if they are not out of temper too. It may possibly have occurred to others as it has to myself, to be present where, on the occasion of an evening party being expected, all the good things for the entertainment had to be made on the afternoon of the same day. I need hardly add that when the guests arrived, neither mistress nor servants were in a very fit state to go through the ceremonial of a dignified reception.

Forethought, then, is a most essential quality in the mistress of a house, if she wishes to maintain throughout her establishment the principle of order. Whatever others *do*, she must *think*. It is not possible for order to exist, where many minds are employed in directing a variety of movements. There must be one presiding intellect to guide the whole; and whether the household to be governed belong to a mansion or a cottage, whether the servants to be directed be many or few, that presiding power must be vested in the mistress, or in some one individual deputed to act in her stead. It is from leaving this thinking and contriving part, along with the executive, to servants, that we see perpetuated so many objectionable and absurd methods of transacting the business of domestic life; methods handed down from one generation to another, and acted upon sometimes with great inconvenience and equal waste, simply because habit has rendered it a sort of established thing, that whatever is done, should be done in a certain manner; for servants are a class of people who think but little, and many of them would rather take double pains, and twice the necessary length of time in doing their work the old way, than risk the experiment of a new one, even if it should ever occur to them to make it.

It must rest with the mistress, then, to introduce improvements and facilities in the transaction of household business; and she will be but little fitted for her office who has not studied before her marriage the best way of doing common and familiar things. Whatever her good intentions, or even her measure of good sense may be, she will labor under painful disadvantages, and difficulties scarcely to be overcome, by taking up this study for the first time after she has become the mistress of a house; for all points of failure here, her own servants will be quick to detect, and most probably not slow to take advantage of.

A married woman thus circumstanced, will certainly act most wisely by studiously concealing her own ignorance; and in order to do this effectually, she must avoid asking foolish questions, at the same time that she watches every thing that is done with careful and quiet scrutiny, so as to learn the how and the why of every trivial act before engaging in it herself, or even venturing a remark upon the manner in which it may be done by others.

But essential as knowledge is to good domestic management, we must ever bear in mind that knowledge is not all. There must be a love of order, a sense of fitness, a quick perception of the appropriateness of time and place, lively impressions of reality and truth, and clear convictions on the subject of relative importance; and in order to the complete qualification of a good wife and mistress, there must be along with all these, not only a willingness, but a strong determination to act upon such impressions and convictions to the full extent of their power to promote social, domestic, and individual happiness.

And if all these requirements are to be classed under the head of order, we must look for those which are still more serious under that of justice.

The word justice has a somewhat startling sound to female ears, and I might perhaps be induced to use a softer expression, could I find one suited to my purpose; though after all, I fancy we should none of us be much the worse for having the word justice, in its simple and imperative strictness, more frequently applied to our relative and social duties. It is, in fact, a good old-fashioned notion, that of doing justice, which has fallen a little too much into disuse; or perhaps, I ought rather to say, has been dismissed from its place among female duties, and considered too exclusively as belonging to points of law and cases of public trial.

I am well aware that justice in its highest sense belongs not to creatures frail, short-sighted, and liable to deception like ourselves; but that strong sense of truth, and honesty, and individual right, which we naturally include in our idea of the love of justice, was surely given us to be exercised in our dealings with each other, and in the general conduct of our domestic affairs. This regard to what is just in itself, necessarily including what is due to others, and what is due from them also, is the moral basis upon which all good management depends; for when once this foundation is removed, an inlet is opened for innumerable lower motives, such as selfishness, vanity, caprice, and a host of others of the same unworthy character, to enter and mix themselves up with the conduct of daily life.

We cannot therefore be too studious to detect, or too prompt to overcome, these enemies to right feeling and to duty; and I believe we shall be best enabled to do this, with the Divine blessing upon our endeavors, by a habit of constantly stretching our ideas to the broad and comprehensive nature of justice in general—justice in its simplicity and its strictness, without deterioration from the influence of custom, and without those qualifications which owe their existence to an artificial state of society.

Imbued with a strong sense of justice, the kind and considerate mistress will see that every member of her household has some rights which others ought not to be allowed to infringe; and if she be attentive to the welfare of her family, she will find sufficient exercise for her love of justice in the settlement of all differences which may arise out of the clashing of individual interests. Even the most insignificant member of such a family, that unfortunate attached to almost all establishments under the name of "the boy," all from him down to the very animals, will have their rights, and such rights can only be consistently maintained by the authority of one presiding mind.

Thus the abuse or the neglect of domestic animals can never prevail to any great extent, where the mistress does her duty; for though servants will sometimes lavish their caresses upon such creatures, they are for the most part careless about their actual wants; and unless properly instructed, and even looked after in this respect, they will sometimes be absolutely cruel. The mistress of a house may thus have an opportunity of teaching her servants, what they possibly will have had no means of learning at home, that these are creatures committed to our care by their Creator and ours, and that we have no more right to practise cruelty upon them, than we have to disobey the righteous law of God in any other respect.

Regarding the important subject of economy in its character of a great moral obligation, rather than simply as an individual benefit, I shall place it under the head of justice; and I do this in the humble hope, that when so classed, it may obtain a greater share of serious attention than could be desired, were the subject to be considered the mere act of saving money. True economy, and that which alone deserves our regard as a study, I have already described as consisting in doing the greatest amount of good with the smallest pecuniary means—not only good to the poor, and to society in general, but good to the family of which we form a part; and of course this study includes the prevention of absolute waste in any department whatever. Such a system of economy, I consider to be entirely distinct from the mere act of saving money; except so far as that all economical persons will endeavor to save money to a certain extent, in order that they or their families may not be dependent upon others. A sense of justice will also induce them to make a suitable provision for those under their care, without doing which they have certainly no right to be generous.

Every thing necessary to the practice of this kind of equitable economy, is consequently necessary to the exercise of justice. We shall therefore turn our attention the more seriously to a few hints on the most commonplace of all subjects—that of saving.

Nor let the refined and fastidious young wife, retaining all her boarding-school contempt for such homely household virtues, dismiss the subject with the hasty conclusion, that such studies are only for the vulgar or the low. There are those who could tell her, that there is a vulgarity in extravagance, of which the really well-bred are seldom guilty; and that no persons are so much addicted to the lavish and indiscriminate waste of money, as those who have been raised from low birth and education to affluent means.

But it is impossible to believe that the sound-minded, honest-hearted, upright women, who form the majority of English wives, should deceive themselves by notions so absurd as these; and I only wish it were possible to embody in the present work, the united evidence of such women in favor of the plans they have themselves found most conducive to the promotion of comfort and economy combined.

I place these two words together, because that can never be called good management, which has not reference to both, or which extracts from the one for the purpose of adding to the other; that can never be called good management, where economy takes precedence of comfort, except only in cases of debt, where comfort ought unquestionably to give place to honesty; and still less can that be called good management where comfort is the only consideration, because the higher consideration of justice must then be neglected.

In order to carry out the principle of justice in her household transactions, it is highly important that the mistress of a family should make herself thoroughly acquainted with the prices and qualities of all common and familiar things, that she may thus be enabled to pay equitably for every thing brought into her house. These are opportunities of observing or violating the laws of justice, which few mistresses have the energy, and still fewer the inclination, to look after themselves; and they are consequently left for the most part to servants and trades-people to adjust as they think proper, each regarding their own interest and convenience, as it is perfectly natural that they should. Servants of course prefer having every article of household consumption brought to the door; and in large towns this is easily managed by small traders in such articles, who can regulate their prices as they think proper, without the cognizance of the mistress of the house, and sometimes without any direct reference to what is the real marketable value of their property. That too much is trusted to interested parties in such cases as these, must be clear to the meanest understanding; for we all know the tendency there is in human nature, to use for selfish purposes the power of doing what is not strictly right, and especially where this can be done without fear of detection.

In the "Daughters of England" I have strongly recommended that young women should cultivate habits of attention to the public as well as the private affairs of the country in which they live, so far as to obtain a general knowledge of its laws and institutions, and of the great political movements taking place around them. The abuse of such knowledge is to make it the basis of party feeling and political animosity; but its proper and legitimate use is that which enables respectable, influential, and patriotic women, to carry out the views of an enlightened legislature through those minor channels which form the connection between public and private life, and the right direction of which is of the utmost importance to the welfare of the country in general.

How little do women, poring over their worsted work, sometimes think of these things! How little do they reflect, that not only is it a part of their duty to govern their household well, but *so* to govern it, that those wise and benevolent enactments designed for the good of the nation at large, which it has been put into the hearts of our rulers to make, may not be frustrated for want of their prompt and willing concurrence! When once this idea has been fully impressed upon the mind of woman, she will not, she cannot, think it a degradation to use every personal effort for the correction of public abuses, rather than it should be said, that while the legislature of England evinced the utmost solicitude for the happiness of the people, there was not patriotism enough among her women to assist in promoting their general good.

But to return to particular instances of domestic economy. The habit of making what are called "cheap bargains," does not appear to me worthy of being classed under this head; because the principle of economy would inspire a wish to pay an equitable and fair price for a good article, rather than a low price for a poor one; and in ninety-nine cases out of a hundred, articles offered for sale as being remarkably cheap, are of very inferior quality.

But above all other things to be guarded against in making bargains, is that of taking advantage of the poor. It is a cruel system carried on by the world, and one against which woman, with her boasted kindness of heart, ought especially to set her face—that of first ascertaining the position, or degree of necessity of the party we deal with, and then offering a price accordingly. Yet, how often do we hear the expression—" I get it done so well, and so cheaply ; for, poor things, they are in such distress, they are glad to do it at any price !"

And a pitiful sight it is to see the plain work, and fine work too, that is done upon such terms. A pitiful thing it is to think of the number of hours which must have been spent, perhaps in the endurance of hunger and cold, before the scanty pittance was earned ; and to compare this with the golden sums so willingly expended at some fashionable milliner's, where, because the lady of the house is *not in want*, the kind-hearted purchaser would be sorry to insult her feelings by offering less.

The same principle applies to ready payment of the poor. It is a mockery of words, to tell them you have no change. The poor know perfectly well that change is to be had ; and when you tell them to call again in a few days, or when it is more convenient to attend to them, perhaps the disappointed applicant goes sorrowing home, to meet the eager glance of a parent, or a child, who has been all day calculating upon some article of food or clothing, which that little payment was expected to have furnished them with the means of procuring.

I am aware that disappointments of this kind are sometimes unavoidable ; but I appeal to my countrywomen, whether as a mere matter of convenience, the poor ought to be sent empty away, when the rich and the independent, because of their greater influence, and the higher respect in which they are held, are paid in a prompt and willing manner, nothing being said either about inconvenience or difficulty.

To all persons, however, whether high or low, rich or poor, it is highly important to good management that frequent payments should be made. Weekly payment of all trades-people is the best, because then neither party has time to forget what has been bought, and they are consequently less likely to make mistakes in their final settlement. As a check upon such mistakes in the making up of accounts, it is indispensable that all bills should be kept for a year at least after their payment ; and though this practice may at first appear useless and troublesome, ample satisfaction will eventually be derived by exemption from all that uncomfortable feeling which arises from uncertainty in this respect—from an idea of having either injured another, or being injured one's self.

There is a foolish habit to which many shopkeepers are addicted, of persuading married women, and particularly the young and inexperienced, to purchase on credit. When they see a lady evidently tempted, looking at an article again and again, and repeatedly asking the price, as if in the hope each time of finding it less, it is perfectly natural in them, if they know the respectability of their customer, to fall in with her weakness, and, accommodating themselves to her inadequate means, to offer the tempting article, to be paid for on some distant day. It is still more foolish, therefore, in the woman who goes unprovided for such a purchase, to trust herself so far as to trifle with temptation ; but the extreme of her folly, is to allow herself to be prevailed upon, at last, to take what she cannot pay for, and probably does not really want.

It is often stated by imprudent women, as an excuse for buying what they do not need, that it was "so extremely cheap ;" but that must always be a dear article to us which we have no use for ; and the money which such things would cost must, in the end, prove more valuable than the cheapest goods which are not necessary, or not calculated to be of use.

Married women who love justice to themselves as well as to others, should always keep strict accounts. Without some evidence of this kind, husbands are sometimes a little incredulous, and such a proof of the right distribution of her means, no one need hesitate to show. While, however, the husband is thus enabled to see for himself what has been the actual expenditure, it must not be supposed that he is qualified to judge in all cases of the necessity for such expenditure being made. The wife alone can do this; and if she enjoys that inestimable blessing to a married woman, her husband's confidence, he will be satisfied that all the rest is right, whether he understands it or not. There is no doubt, if he was consulted about every purchase to be made, he would think in some instances that the article could be done without; while in others, he would probably choose a far more expensive one than was necessary. A wise and prudent woman will, therefore, so manage these affairs, as to obtain the privilege of having them left entirely to her judgment.

She will find too, that economy does not consist so much in buying little, as in buying suitably; for a house or a wardrobe may be so scantily supplied, that each article has to do the service of many, and is thus prematurely worn out, or effectually destroyed, by being put to uses for which it never was designed. The poor girl who has but a thin pair of shoes, and no money to buy stronger, must unavoidably destroy them in one day's journey; when, had they been used only for proper purposes, they might have lasted a year. And it is the same with a scantily furnished kitchen. Absolute waste to a very great extent must necessarily be the consequence of having but few implements for daily use, and making them serve every purpose as occasion may require. With the best supply of kitchen utensils, however, their selection and use ought not to be left entirely to servants. The mistress herself must sometimes direct in this department, unless she would see the amount of her bills alarmingly increased by the habit most servants have, of snatching up what is nearest to them, rather than thinking what is fittest to be used. The same rule applies to household linen,

of which an ample supply, given out with regularity and judgment, will always be found most economical in the end. But on no account whatever let any deficiency in this department, or in that of your kitchen, be supplied by borrowing. There is no occasion for the defects of your establishment to be made known to others, and, except in cases of extraordinary emergency, if you cannot afford to purchase what is wanted, the sooner you learn to do without it the better.

With regard to food, too, I am inclined to think that to have a table comfortably supplied with a moderate variety of dishes, is by no means inconsistent with the strictest economy. I have sometimes even fancied that a spare dinner had the effect of producing a very disproportionate appetite; at least I remember, when a girl, having occasionally the privilege of sitting down to a table of this kind, when I always felt most perversely inclined to eat up every thing that was set before me.

But leaving this fact to be settled by political economists, it must be allowed that persons in general are not so childish as to eat more, because they see more; and in the appearance of a well-supplied table, there is an air of comfort and respectability, which under ordinary circumstances, I cannot think we should derive any advantage from giving up. Besides which, a certain extent of variety affords opportunity for bringing out again, in a more attractive form, many things which must have been otherwise dismissed altogether. In this art the French have arrived at great perfection; and as a proof of the correctness of these observations, the cheapness of their way of living is always a subject of surprise to the English, on their first acquaintance with French habits.

Still, we must feel that the system is a dangerous one, when it leads to excess; far better—far better is it to eat the last morsel of plain food prepared every day, than to give the time, and the thoughts, too much to the preparation and enjoyment of food.

But the great point to be observed, both in the study and the practice of economy, is to proportion your expenditure to your means. The difference, even of a hundred a year, in the income of a family, makes a considerable difference in the duties of the mistress with regard to economy. Thus, it may be highly meritorious for one married woman to do all her needlework herself, while, in another, it would evince a disregard for the fitness of things, to spend her time in doing what she would be more in the way of her duty to employ the poor and the needy to do for her.

In all these cases, it is evident that principle, rather than inclination, must form the basis of our actions; and in following out the principle of justice more especially, that self must hold a very inferior place in our calculations. The same may be said of those duties which follow, and which are comprised under the head of benevolence; for though selfishness and generosity may, in the first view, appear to be directly opposite in their nature, the act of giving is, in many cases, only the gratification of a refined selfishness, with which the principle of integrity has to wage determined war. Thus there can be no generosity in giving what is not, strictly speaking, our own, nor justice in receiving thanks for what we had no right to give.

To be solicitous either to give, or to receive, costly presents in your own family, is a sort of childish weakness, and particularly to expect such presents from a husband, for where there is a perfect identity of feeling and possession, both as regards money and goods, the wife may just as well purchase the valuable article for herself. There is, however, something gratifying to every heart in being remembered during absence; but the gratification consists rather in finding that our trifling wants have been thought of and supplied, than that the indulgence of our self-love or our vanity has had to be taken into account; and a thimble in such a case may be more valuable than a costly gem.

The married woman, as soon as she takes upon herself the responsibility of standing at the head of an establishment, should withdraw herself in a great measure from those little obligations and kindnesses, which as a young woman and unmarried, she might with propriety have received. She must, therefore, strictly avoid courting such favors, especially from the great, remembering that in being the mistress of a house, she has herself become a source from whence kindness ought to flow, and consequently is not so proper an object for receiving it.

To be "just before we are generous," is a good old maxim. The duties of benevolence must, therefore, always be made subservient to those of integrity. But still, where a family is neither in debt, nor in want of the common necessaries of life, there must be something due from such a family to those who are more needy than themselves.

It is a privilege we all enjoy, of being at liberty to choose our own way of being charitable; yet if we think seriously on the subject of giving, as a duty, and regard our means as only lent to us for the purpose of doing the greatest possible amount of good which they are capable of effecting; we shall find that instead of its being the mere indulgence of a natural impulse, to give, it is often the study of a lifetime to learn how to give judiciously.

To judge by the frequency of its practice, one would suppose that one of the most approved methods of serving the poor, was to give away at the door pieces of broken or otherwise objectionable food. Yet I am disposed to think that, upon the whole, more harm than good results from this practice; for, to say nothing of the temptation it offers to the poor to exaggerate their own wants and sufferings, the temptation to servants is no trifling one, to be perpetually adding to the charitable hoard, what a little ingenuity or care might have converted into a wholesome or palatable dish. Besides which it is impossible that any family should be able to furnish a regular supply of such food, and the disappointment of the really destitute must be very great, on those days when they are obliged to return home to set down to an empty table, or perhaps to go supperless to bed. In addition to which objections, we may safely add, that the fewer supplicants and hangers-about, to be found at our doors, the better. Those are seldom the most needy who ask assistance in this way, and happily for our benevolence, there are innumerable channels now open, through which we may at least endeavor to do good with less probability of doing harm.

In the exercise of kindness to the poor, care is often necessary to avoid falling into popular mistakes with regard to the merit of certain cases, which after all frequently consists in nothing more than a few circumstances of interest attaching to them. The tide of fashion, when it takes a charitable course, will sometimes pour a perfect flood of benefits upon certain individuals, to the neglect of others equally deserving, and perhaps more in need. But the mistress of a family, whose mind is well governed, will be her own judge in such matters, and not allowing either indolence or self-indulgence to stand in her way, nor even deputing the task to others, she will, as far as it is possible to do so, examine the case for herself, in order that she may not be led away by the partial statements or highly colored representations of her friends.

For all the purposes of benevolence, she will also keep a separate provision, and separate accounts, in order to ascertain at the end of the year, or at any particular time, what has been the exact proportion of her resources thus distributed. Without this kind of record, we are apt sometimes to fancy we have been more generous than is really the case; or, on the other hand, we may have been liberal beyond what was just, for it is not the number of cases we relieve, which has to be considered, so much as the due proportion of our means which is bestowed upon charitable purposes.

When the duty of benevolence, extended through offices of charity, is considered in this light, as being no duty in some cases, and in others one of serious extent and responsibility, and thus bearing, through all the intermediate degrees between these two extremes, exact reference to our pecuniary means, to our situation in life, and to the number of relative claims we have to fulfil, it will easily be seen, that to lay down any precise rules for the amount of money which ought to be expended in charity, would be presuming upon an extent of knowledge which no single individual can possess. Besides which, there are so many ways of doing good, that benevolent feeling can often find free exercise through channels which could scarcely be considered as belonging to what is generally understood by charity.

But while perfectly aware that little can be done in the way of benefiting our fellow-creatures, without regard to their spiritual welfare, I own I am one of those who would wish that the bodies, as well as the souls of the poor might be cared for; nor can I think they would be less likely to attend to instruction, for being comfortably clothed and sufficiently fed.

The mistress of a family, when truly benevolent, will not rest satisfied with merely giving to the poor. She will visit them in their dwellings, make herself acquainted with their habits, characters, and circumstances: and while urging upon them their religious duties, or recommending such means of religious instruction as may be within their reach, her own experience in the practice of economy will enable her occasionally to throw in a few useful hints on the best method of employing their scanty means, so as that every thing may be turned to the most useful account. Assistance of this kind, judiciously and kindly given, is often more valuable than money would be without it; and those who have but little to give, may often, by such means, extend their influence to as wide a circle of usefulness, as if they had thousands at their disposal.

The indigent and the suffering are often good judges of what is real, and what is pretended sympathy, or of what is meant for kindness, without sympathy at all. Thus the most sincere and fervent zeal for their spiritual improvement often fails to produce any effect, simply from the fact of little attention being paid to their temporal affairs, or only such as they can perceive at once to be unaccompanied by any feeling of sympathy. It is a happy constitution of mind, therefore, which has been given to woman, no doubt for holy and benevolent purposes, which enables her with a quick and sensitive feeling to enter into all the minutiæ of daily experience, without interruption to those higher aims which must occupy the supreme attention of every Christian woman in her intercourse with those who are brought under her influence or her care.

The advantages of adaptation are never more felt than in our association with the poor. By a look or a tone, they may be attracted or repelled. Yet how little do some worthy people think of this, when they speak to the poor in an authoritative, or disrespectful manner! It is good to bear about with us the remembrance of this fact—that we have no more right to be rude to the poor than to the rich. Even as regards household servants, so strong is the feeling of that class of persons in this respect, that I believe mistresses who never deviate from a proper manner of speaking themselves, have seldom occasion to complain that their servants speak improperly to them.

In every mistress of a family, the poor of her immediate neighborhood should feel that they have a friend, and where the principle of benevolence has been strongly implanted in the heart, such a mistress will esteem this consideration too high a privilege to allow any regard for mere personal interest to interfere with the just discharge of so sacred a trust. Yet to befriend the poor substantially, and with reference to their ultimate good, all who have made the experiment will allow to be a difficult, as well as a sacred duty, requiring much patience, forbearance, and equanimity of mind, with much confidence in a superintending Providence, and faith in Him who chose his own disciples among the poor.

That benevolence which commences its career with high expectations of reward in this world, is sure to be withered by disappointment. Indeed, there is so much to discourage the exercise of charity for the sake of producing great and conspicuous results, that most persons who begin upon this principle, end by having their temper soured, their confidence destroyed, and their minds embittered by uncharitable feelings towards their fellow-creatures in general. "The poor are so ungrateful," is their frequent remark—"so dishonest, so requiring; there is no pleasure in doing any thing for them." But how different is the spirit which prompts these complaints, from that of the Bible, where the poor are mentioned in almost every page, and where the duty of kindness and consideration towards them is enforced upon the simple ground of their being *poor*, without regard to any other merit or demerit whatever!

Nor is it to the poor alone, but towards her fellow-creatures in general, that the woman who undertakes the superintendence of a family, should cultivate feelings of kindness and benevolence. Men, engaged in the active affairs of life, have neither time nor opportunity for those innumerable little acts of consideration which come within the sphere of female duty, nor are they by nature so fitted as woman for entering into the peculiarities of personal feeling, so as to enable them to sympathize with the suffering or the distressed. But woman, in the happiest exercise of her natural endowments, enjoys all those requisites which are combined in a real friend; and as such she ought always to be regarded at the head of her domestic establishment—a friend with whom all within the reach of her influence may feel that their interests are safe—a friend in whose sympathy all may share, and in whose charity all may find a place. No one, however, can be such a friend as this, without having cultivated benevolent dispositions towards the human race in general, without feeling that all are members of one great family, only differently placed for a short period of their existence, and that all are objects of kindness and care to the same heavenly Father.

CHAP. XI.

TREATMENT OF SERVANTS AND DEPENDANTS.

IF, as soon as a woman marries, she has the services of domestic assistants at her command, she has also devolving upon her the responsibility of their comfort and their general welfare ; and it is a serious thought that she cannot, by any means, escape from this responsibility, whatever may, in other respects, be the privileges and indulgences of her situation. Neither the affection of her husband nor the kindness of her friends can do any thing to relieve her here, except only so far as their advice may aid her judgment; but as the mistress of a house she must be the one responsible being for the habits, and, in a great measure, for the circumstances of those who are placed under her care.

By the thoughtless or inexperienced it may be asked how this should be, since servants are expected to care for us, not we for them ? Such, however, is not the language of a Christian woman, with whom it will be impossible to forget that her influence and example must unavoidably give a tone to the character of her whole household ; and if there be no solicitude for a bias to be given towards what is good, it must unavoidably be towards what is evil. It is morally impossible that it should be neither one way nor the other, because the very time which a servant spends beneath a master's roof, will, of necessity, be confirming old habits, if not spent in acquiring new ones ; and thus while fondly persuading yourself that because you are doing nothing you cannot be doing harm, you may, in reality, be guilty of the sin of omission, which, in cases of moral responsibility, is often of the most serious consequence.

It is too frequently considered that servants are a class of persons merely subject to our authority. Could we regard them more as placed under our influence, we should take a wider and more enlightened view of our own responsibilities with regard to them. And after all, it is influence rather than authority which governs a household ; not but

that every mistress has a right to expect implicit obedience, all neglect of which is injurious to both the parties concerned, and in order to enforce which, her orders should always be given in as clear and decided a manner as possible, leaving nothing, except where it is absolutely necessary, to contingencies, and nothing to the choice of the servant herself, unless good reasons should be adduced for a change of purpose ; and then the orders of the mistress should be so worded as to make the purpose her own, and not to allow the servant an opportunity of feeling that she has overruled the plans of her mistress, and in reality substituted her own.

Where the mistress is an ignorant one, these points of observance are very difficult to maintain, and the habit of giving foolish orders, inconvenient or impossible to be executed, and of finding that her servant is capable of proposing what is at once more reasonable and much to be preferred, will, in all probability, reduce her to a mere nonentity as regards authority in her kitchen, and may ultimately be the cause of her withdrawing from all interference there.

But necessary as it is that a mistress should be implicitly obeyed, I repeat, that it is not by mere authority that a household can be well governed ; because there are innumerable ways in which servants can deceive without being detected, and carry on their own schemes while they appear to be adopting those of a mistress ; it is, therefore, by no other means than by the establishment of mutual feelings of confidence and respect, that we can hope to be as faithfully served when absent, as when inspecting our affairs in person ; and as I have already said that a kitchen can never be the proper element for an enlightened woman to live in, the greater confidence she feels in a right system being carried on there, the more leisure she will possess for other avocations, and the more happiness she will enjoy.

The question then arises, how is this right understanding, and this perfect confidence to be attained ? I answer, first, by respecting the rights of servants, and secondly, by atten-

their interests. There are certain
which you have a right to require of
nd among them is implicit obedience ;
re are also many things which even
they might greatly promote your con-
:e, you have no right to require. You
) right to require a reduction of wages
what you first agreed to give, or in-
ny deviation from what was stipulated
hat agreement. And here it may be
observe, that all particular require-
with regard to dress and personal
should be mentioned at that time, so
disappointments or disputes may af-
ls arise. Notes should also be made
1 arrangements, with the time of hir-
d the rate of wages : and when all
iings in the beginning are clearly stated,
ly understood, it may tend greatly to
vention of unpleasant consequences.
itever your own circumstances may
i the right of your servants to have a
 incy of rest, and of wholesome food ;
'en in cases of sickness, or other exi-
you have no right to *require* that either
be given up ; to request it as a kind-
i the only proper manner in which a
t should be brought to make such con-
s ; and we have often a beautiful ex-
for imitation in the perfect willingness
/hich, when thus treated, they will de-
emselves personal indulgence, more
illy sit up night after night with the
ithout in the intermediate times neg-
their daily work.
a delicate part of good management,
very important one in maintaining in-
i, to keep always clear distinctions on
points, and not even to *demand* the
from the servant's bed, remembering
l things essential to their daily suste-
and nightly rest, have been stipulated
our first agreement, and that your ser-
are consequently under no greater ob-
1 than other members of your family,
) up what may be classed under the
f bed or board. But I must again ob-
that there is a manner of *requesting*
things to be done, when required on

any extraordinary occasion, which seldom
meets with a refusal, or even with an unwilling compliance.

A certain degree of care of your servants'
health is a species of kindness which they
always feel gratefully, and which is no more
than ought to be shown by the mistress towards every member of her household. Indeed it is impossible to imagine a kind-hearted
woman neglecting the pallid looks, and lan-
guid movements of those who are spending
their strength in her service ; and if she be
at the same time a lover of justice, she will
remember that the bodily exercise necessary
for carrying on household labor during the
day, requires a greater interval of rest than
such occupations as are generally carried on
in the drawing-room. Instead of which, how
often do we find those on whom devolves
the burden of this labor, required to rise two
or three hours earlier than their mistress,
and kept up at night as late as any of the
household !—kept up perhaps to wait for
the return of visitors, when another member
of the family, allowed to rest longer in the
morning, might as well have done so in their
stead—kept up on a cold winter's night to
warm a bed, which the indulgent occupant
might more properly have warmed herself,
unless she had chosen to retire earlier—or
kept up perhaps until a late hour for family
worship ; a practice which requires no further comment, than to say, that except on
very extraordinary occasions, or where great
allowance is made in the morning for rest,
no servants ought to be expected to attend
family worship after ten at night.

By allowing, and even requiring your servants to retire early, you have a right to expect their services early in the morning,
without which, no household can be properly
conducted ; for when the day commences
with hurry and confusion in order to over-
take lost time, the same state of things, only
aggravated by its unavoidable tendency to
call forth evil tempers, impatient expressions,
and angry retorts, will in all probability continue until the end of the day. And here we
see, as in thousands of instances besides, the

importance of making ourselves acquainted with what belongs to nature, and especially that of the human heart. We may compel an outward observance of the laws we lay down for our own families, but we cannot compel such feelings to go along with their observance, as alone can render it of any lasting benefit either to our servants or ourselves. Thus by rendering our service an irksome one, or in other words, not attending to what the constitution of human nature requires, we effectually destroy our good influence; and if by bringing religion into the same hard service, we render it an irksome restraint, the mischief we do by this means may be as fearful in its extent, as it is serious and important in its character. But of this, more in another chapter.

The same care which is exercised with regard to your servants' health, should be extended to their habits in general, and even to cases in which their good alone is concerned; for it is an act of injustice to complain of the habits of this class of persons, without doing your part to form, upon better principles, those which come within the sphere of your influence. It is often objected to this duty, that nothing can be done for the good of young servants, so long as they are encouraged at home in what is foolish and wrong. The mothers then are clearly to blame; and certainly the mothers in many poor families are bad enough. But who made the mothers what they are, or helped to make them so? Unquestionably the negligent, injudicious, or unprincipled mistresses under whose influence their early lives were spent.

And have you not then sufficient regard for the welfare of future generations to begin a new system, by which the errors of the last may be corrected? For the little thoughtless girl just entering beneath your roof—the young nursery-maid—she of whom nobody thinks, except to find fault when she has done wrong—she who perhaps never thinks herself, except to contrive how she shall manage to purchase a ribbon like that upon her mistress's cap—this very girl is gradually experiencing under your influence, and, nominally at least, under your care, that great and important change of thought, feeling, and habit, which is not improperly called the formation of character; and this girl will consequently take away with her whatever bias she receives either from your neglect, or your attentions, first into other families, and then into her own, where she herself will probably in her turn have to train up children both for this world and the next.

Will the wives of England then think me very extravagant in my notions of what is due towards servants, when I propose to those in the middle class of society, that as Christian women they should consider such young servants as placed peculiarly under their care; because it is only by beginning early, that that great and radical change can be effected in the habits and character of servants generally, which all unite in considering as so urgently required.

If a mistress would really do this, and I cannot see how any responsible person so circumstanced is justified in neglecting it, she would consider that some oversight of her servants' wardrobe was absolutely necessary; and as they grow older, and come to be intrusted with money of their own, the same oversight should extend to their manner of spending it. It is an excellent thing when servants are allowed time for making their own clothes, and it is no mean occupation for the mistress of a house to teach them how to do so. I speak on the supposition that she is acquainted with this art herself, for I cannot imagine the education of an English woman in the middle class of society complete, without her having become familiar with the art of making every article of dress she wears. Not that she is under any obligation to continue the practice of making her own clothes; that is a totally different matter; but as this class of women are situated, and taking into account all the probabilities of change of circumstance, failure of health, or failure of pecuniary means, I am convinced that no one could have to regret, while thousands might have to rejoice, at having acquired in early life an art so capable of being made useful both to themselves and others.

I believe that one half of the forlornness, discomfort, and apparent destitution of the poor around us, arises, not so much from absolute want of means, as from the absence of all knowledge of this kind. They are unfortunately but too ready to imitate us in our love of finery, our extravagance, and self-indulgence; and it is a serious question whether they discover any thing else in us which they can imitate; but let them see our economy, our industry, our contrivance, and our solicitude to turn every thing to the best account, and I believe they would not be slow to imitate these habits as well as the others.

The art of mending, for instance, though most important to the poor, is one in which they are lamentably deficient; and so much waste, disorder, and slovenliness, are the consequence of not being able to mend skilfully, that this department of neatness and economy is one in which all young servants should be carefully instructed; more especially as the making-up of new clothes is a much easier, as well as generally more agreeable task, than that of mending old ones, so that they look respectable to the last.

By this kind of oversight of her servants' wardrobe, a kind-hearted and judicious mistress may easily obtain some direction in the expenditure of their money, and in nothing is assistance to the poorer classes more necessary than in this. Servants generally are pleased to have the approbation of a beloved and respected mistress in those cases over which she does not assume any direct authority; and they would be equally mortified to find they had incurred her disapprobation by the purchase of what was worthless, or unbefitting their situation. By this means, too, mistresses would generally be better able than they are, to understand what is sufficient, and consequently what is just, with regard to wages; for while, on the one hand, some require their servants always to look respectable without allowing them the means to do so, others are induced by fashion or custom

to give higher wages than are really any benefit to the receiver.

But the variety of instances are too numerous to specify, in which the Christian care and oversight of a good mistress may be invaluable to a young servant. I will mention but one more, and that of greater importance than any which have yet fallen under our consideration. I mean the preservation of young servants from circumstances of exposure or temptation.

Those who have never lived in large towns, and especially in London, would scarcely give credit to the facts, were they told the number of instances in which servants are brought from the country, and being obliged, from illness or some other cause, to leave their employers, are allowed to be cast upon the mercy of the public, friendless and destitue, and too often a prey to the cruel deceptions which are practised upon young females thus situated. Some of the most painful among the many distressing circumstances which come under the notice of those Christian ladies who have the oversight of female penitentiaries, are cases in which country servants have been brought to town, and having lost their health, or suffered from accident, have been placed in hospitals, and left there without regard to their future destiny; when, on coming out, they have found that all clue was lost to their former masters or mistresses, and that they were consequently alone in the streets of London, without money, without friends, and without the knowledge of any respectable place in which they might find shelter.

It may be said that these are extreme cases, but it is lamentably true that these, and others of similar neglect, are not so rare as persons would suppose who are unacquainted with the practices of our large towns.

Another evil against which mistresses ought to be especially on their guard, is the introduction of unprincipled char-women, or other assistants, into their families. In the country it is comparatively easy to ascertain what is the general moral character of those around us; but in large towns this knowledge is more difficult to acquire, and incalculable mischief has often been the consequence of associating young servants with persons of this description.

The practice of sending out young female servants late at night, to bring home any members of the family who may be out visiting, or placing them in any other manner unnecessarily in circumstances of exposure, are considerations to which we ought not to be indifferent; and the mistress who allows her servant to be thus circumstanced, would do well to ask herself how she would like a young sister, or a daughter, to be placed in a similar situation. Can it be that youth has not as strong a claim to our protection in the lower as in the higher walks of life? Can it be that innocence is not as precious to the poor as to the rich? Did the case admit of any degree of comparison, I should say that it was more so; for what has a poor girl but her character to depend upon? Or when once the stigma of having deviated from the strict line of propriety attaches to her name, who is there to defend her from the consequences? Her future lot will in all probability be to become the wife of some poor and hard-working man, whose whole amount of worldly wealth will be comprised in the respectability of his humble home. Who then, through indifference or neglect, would allow a shadow to steal in, still less a blight to fall, where, in spite of poverty, in spite of trial, in spite of all those hardships which are the inevitable portion of the man who earns his bread by the labor of his hands, his home might still be an earthly paradise to him?

Young women of a higher grade in society, or those who are more properly called ladies, being all taught in the great school of polished society, acquire the same habits of decorum, and even of modesty, to a certain extent; and the restrictions of society rendering it more painful to deviate from such habits, than to maintain them through life, we come, very naturally, to look upon them rather as a matter of course than as a merit.

But in the modesty of a poor young girl there is inexpressible beauty, because we know that it must arise from the right feelings of her heart; and none who are capable of truly estimating this charm, would for the wealth of worlds be the cause of its being lost.

It is a common saying with servants, that they do not fear work if well treated; and I believe such little acts of consideration as the heart of a kind mistress will naturally suggest, may be made to go much further in stimulating them to a right performance of their duty, than either high wages or great personal indulgence. A little consideration shown for their wishes, where the matter is one of little moment to their employers, is felt by them as a real kindness, and often abundantly rewarded by their willingness and alacrity in doing whatever is required of them.

An instance was once brought painfully under my notice, where the mistress of a house and some of her family were consulting about whether a servant should be sent to a neighboring town before, or after, dinner. They themselves appearing to have no choice, it was suggested by another party, that the servant would prefer going in the afternoon. "He prefer it, indeed!" exclaimed the lady of the house; "then for that reason he shall go in the morning." When it is added, that the lady was a most kind, and in many respects, truly excellent character, this fact is difficult to believe; and I am only induced to state it as a striking proof to what an extent benevolent feeling may be restrained in its exercise, by the habit of thinking that servants are merely passive instruments upon which authority ought to be exercised; and that, consequently, all pretension on their part to an equality of feeling with ourselves, as regards what is agreeable or otherwise, ought to be put down by the most prompt and decided measures.

After all, however, it must be allowed, that there are some servants, and perhaps not a few, who cannot, by the best and most judicious treatment, be moulded to our wishes; and with regard to these, if the case is a decided one, that they can neither do good to us, nor we to them, the sooner we get rid of them the better. Before deciding too hastily to part with a servant, we should, however, call into exercise all the charity we can, by remembering how different their education and early treatment have been from ours, and if we cannot on this ground forgive them some faults, either they or we must be wrong indeed.

Again, there may have been faults on our side as well as theirs. We may have been too lax in our discipline, for kindness ceases to be such when it degenerates into negligence. Thus, to permit servants to feel that there are in your household departments of duty which you never superintended, and places and things secure from your inspection, is allowing them a license which few are so conscientious as not, in some measure, to abuse. It may happen too, that you have been expecting regularity from them, while you have failed to practise it yourself; or, that you have been requiring neatness, order, and punctuality, when your own example, on these points of observance, has been far from corresponding with your precepts and injunctions.

That care should be exercised not to part too hastily with servants, is as much for the interest of one party as another; since the distinction of a bad name as a mistress, is sure to be felt in its natural consequence of preventing good servants seeking employment under such direction. It is in the power of all mistresses to make it a privilege to live with them; but still, even this privilege will occasionally be abused. There are cases too, in which the natural dispositions of the two parties are not suited; and there is such a thing as a mistress becoming afraid of her servant—afraid to thwart her plans, or afraid to enforce others; and where such is the feeling, whatever may be the excellences of the servant, that she is not in her proper place with such a mistress, is sufficiently evident.

Instances of dishonesty, or other cases of serious moral delinquency, I have not deem-

ed it necessary to mention, because all must be aware of the importance of treating them in an equitable and summary manner. The only thing to be observed in relation to these is, that the evidence upon which we act should be clear and decisive.

In all cases of dissatisfaction, it is good to bear in mind the familiar and true maxim, that " good mistresses make good servants ;" and that with persons who are constantly changing, some fault must rest with themselves—some fault attributable either to mismanagement or neglect—some fault arising either from too great indulgence, or too great severity, or perhaps from a mixture of both. And I am strongly disposed to think, that independently of such faults, many of the grievances we complain of in our domestic affairs, and especially those which arise out of the foolish, perverse, or unprincipled conduct of our servants, might be obviated by more careful attention being paid to the formation of their character when young.

That a better system is also required with regard to the practice of giving characters to servants, is universally allowed ; yet few persons seem to have the moral courage to begin with a plan, which shall at once be more just to the employers and the employed. This weakness of purpose originates, no doubt, in an amiable feeling of anxiety, lest, by speaking of our servants as we have really found them, we should deprive them of a future home. The case unquestionably has its difficulties, yet as a moral obligation, it must be allowed, that the sooner we begin to act fairly and honestly, the better it will ultimately be, both for ourselves and those with whom we are associated ; and there can be no doubt, that the confidence all servants feel in being able to obtain what is called a character, so long as they have not been really dishonest, insolent, or disobedient, renders them more careless than they otherwise would be, of those minor points of domestic duty, which, taken as a whole, form an aggregate of considerable importance to those who engage their services. This, then, is one of those cases, in which the Wives of

England are called upon to assist each other, not only in making a strong determination, but in acting upon it, so far as to break through a popular and long-established practice, by speaking of servants, when asked for their character, in such terms as they really deserve; without reference to their worldly interests, or indeed to any thing but the simple truth. If by such means a few of them should be longer than they now are in obtaining situations, a great many would be more careful to fill their places to the satisfaction of the families by whom they are employed; and thus honesty would be found in the end, as it always is, to be the best policy.

In addition to household servants, many married women have devolving upon them the serious responsibility of caring for apprentices, or other assistants in the way of business; and in the discharge of these duties, it is most important for all who are thus circumstanced to ask themselves, whether they are acting upon the golden rule of doing to others what they would that others should do to them, or to those in whom they are most warmly interested. If they are, their merit is great, and there can be no doubt but their reward will be so too; for we must all allow, that it requires no ordinary share of kind feeling, or of Christian principle, to do all which a high sense of duty requires in this respect.

There are many reasons why the task is difficult—almost too difficult for mere human nature to perform; and it is not the least of these, that most young men who begin to learn a business, enter as strangers into a family at an age when they have little to recommend them as companions, except to their own associates, or to a partial parent; yet at that precise time of their lives, when the formation of their habits and character requires the strictest care. It is easy to imagine that few women would prefer spending much of their time with youths of fifteen, or eighteen years of age, in connection with whom they have no family tie, or strong connecting interest; but why, on the other hand,

the wife of a man who is engaged in business, to the successful pursuit of which she owes all her pecuniary advantages, should hold herself above her husband's clerks or apprentices, I never could distinctly see; more especially as time was when her own husband was thus situated, and most probably time will be, when her sons will be the same.

Is it possible, then, that a mother thus circumstanced can look with indifference to the future, when the happy boy who plays beside her, the joy of her own heart, and the pride of his father's—the spirited handsome fellow who carries away the prizes at his school, and lords it over his playmates, and only softens into tenderness when he sees his mother's tears—is it possible that she can think with indifference of the time when he shall be old enough to go out into a stranger's family—nay, actually be bound there for a term of years, and thus inwrought as it were with the entire fabric of a new order of domestic arrangements, yet notwithstanding all this, made to sit apart, and to feel that he is not only an alien but an absolute intruder, as regards the mistress of that family and her friends? Could the fond mother follow her boy when thus circumstanced up to his own bedroom in the attic, and see how often, for want of a welcome at the household hearth, he sits there upon his box, and reads the books he brought from home, at the risk of being chidden for the light he has kept burning;—could she see the far-off way in which he sits at the family board, satisfying his hunger according to necessity, not choice;—could she see the manner in which, from the very overflow of the life of his young spirit he is driven down and compelled to make merry with associates unfitted to himself, at least to that self with which he was identified in his father's home, but which he has almost ceased to remember now;—could she hear when he speaks how his voice is becoming gradually habituated to the utterance of low thoughts and words which never formed a part of the language of his home;—but beyond all this—could she see his Sabbaths—

his days of rest—those happy days, when the members of his father's family used all to be united in equality of feeling, and solicitous only to give precedence to each other,—could she behold him walking the streets of some great town, and for want of home-attractions, for want of cordiality and welcome at his master's fireside, familiarizing himself with the sinful practices of others similarly circumstanced;—could the mother, beholding all this, trace out its fearful and degrading consequences upon the future destiny of her boy, she would be ready to exclaim to the mistress of that household—"Save my child!"

Should any such appeal be made, the mistress of that family would in all probability reply with indignation—"The young men employed in my husband's business enjoy the very best of food, they are not required to work beyond the hours agreed upon, and their sleeping-rooms are healthy and well furnished." And all this may be strictly true, yet the mother's heart may be unsatisfied, for she knows, and we all know, that it is possible to be well cared for as regards the body, and yet be made to feel most destitute. We all know that there is a kind of treatment which elevates the moral feelings, and another which degrades them, rendering the spirit upon which it operates, grovelling, servile, mean. And if this powerful influence should be made to weigh upon, and bear down the buoyant mind of youth, what must we expect, after such treatment, will be the downward tendency of old age?

But is it possible, we ask again, that the mother whose natural instinct renders her so keenly alive to all these feelings as regards her own child, can be insensible to the claims of others?—can be induced by her own pride or her own selfishness to trample under foot the high moral obligation laid upon her, to be as a mother to her own household, but especially to the young, remembering that they will go forth into the world bearing the seal upon their foreheads of her maternal care, or of her most culpable neglect? Nor is this all. She must remember, too, that these very youths are to constitute in after

life that strong phalanx of respectability, in whose moral power are vested the interests of the people, and the welfare of the state. Is it right then—is it just—is it politic—that during five or seven long years of the lives of such men—years in which the most lasting impressions they ever will receive, are made upon their minds—is it right, or in any way to be reconciled to English women, that for this portion of their lives they should be subjected to a system of moral discipline, calculated, in almost every way, to lower them as future citizens of the world?

But it is not always thus. There are noble and beautiful instances of women who absolutely could not live upon such terms; warm-hearted, patriotic women, who cannot sit down to their own tables without a cordial welcome for every one entitled to a place at the same board—who, putting aside all personal feeling, can even make friends of such associates, remembering that to their parents and their country they are in a great measure responsible for the high or low position such men may take in after life. Yes, we are happy in believing there are those who would willingly bear all the annoyance or restraint of such society, were it tenfold greater than it is, rather than be the cause of one young man being drawn out from home to seek enjoyment, or down into a lower grade of social fellowship, for a freedom and a cordiality which he could not find with her.

Contemptuously as young men will often speak of the influence and the habits of women in general, I believe there are few who may not in the early part of their lives, be more easily influenced by women than by men—by judicious women, I mean, for, notwithstanding the absurdities of which some youths are guilty themselves, they appear to be instinctively quick-sighted to the absurdities of others, and especially to those of woman. In fact, they seem glad to lay hold of any excuse for despising them, and, even where they feel the greatest respect, will seldom acknowledge it openly or directly. But for all this, the cautious and well-ordered treatment of women tells upon their characters in the end ; and by a little good-natured falling-in with their humors, a little forbearance under the infliction of their annoyances, a little good sense, and a great deal of cheerfulness, an amiable woman will seldom fail to obtain, even without the assumption of any direct authority, an extensive influence over the young men with whom she is associated.

For this reason, and because the master of a family with whom it rests to exercise real authority cannot so well unbend, and make himself familiar with the young people under his direction, the claims of this part of the community are strong upon the wives of England, who as they value the comfort of their own sons, and estimate with regard to them the advantages of a high moral standard, can surely not forget the interests of the stranger's son committed to their care.

The same observations apply with equal force to dependants of every description, excepting only that those who are not bound, may be considered as at liberty to find situations more suited to their ideas of comfort.

But, above all others, the class of destitute or homeless relatives are most entitled to our consideration and kindness. Yet such is the weakness of human nature in cases of severe or protracted trial, that the good and the happiness of all parties seem to require as little mixing up as possible in the same household, of rich and poor relations. When the poor have to be provided for by more affluent relatives, it is better—far better, to do this at a distance, or at least not associated as one family ; though such needful precaution has nothing whatever to do with the kindness which may often be most appropriately extended towards them as guests, or indeed as members of the same family for a limited period.

In all such cases, there are difficulties to be contended with on both sides, owing to the natural tendency in one party to suspect or imagine slights, and in the other to apprehend or resist encroachments. One half of these, however, I am fully persuaded, might be obviated by a candid and delicate mode of behavior on the part of the mistress of a house who entertains such relatives as guests. Her behavior must be delicate in the extreme, because she has to do with those whose peculiar situation renders them more than commonly susceptible of pain : and it must be candid ; because in all such cases the habit of leaving things to be understood is the surest way to produce misunderstandings. Still, the delicacy which would make no difference be felt, would fail in its object to do good ; because as the world considers there is a vast difference between abundant and slender pecuniary means, there could be no kindness in persuading those who are but scantily supplied in this respect, that they are to mix in society upon the same terms as the rich ; and more especially after one or more generations have marked this difference between them and their relatives by stronger characters.

While it is left to all persons to decide according to their own judgment to what extent they will cultivate the acquaintance of their poorer relatives, the manner of doing this admits of no doubt ; for to receive them as guests without a welcome, is at once a breach of justice and of hospitality. The welcome then which I would earnestly recommend, is one which sets them perfectly at ease as to any fear of intrusion, and which does away with all idea that personally they are considered as inferiors by the mistress of the house ; though at the same time her behavior should be such as to assist them in marking out for their safety, in associating with others, those delicate distinctions, upon the nice observance of which so much of their comfort and respectability depends. By encouraging them to trust implicitly to her candor in expressing her wishes respecting them, she may, as the mistress of a house, be enabled to become a real friend to a class of persons whose claims are perhaps the strongest of any upon our sympathy and consideration. For let the case be our own —let the lapse of time as it passes over our family connections leave us alone to struggle with a tide of adverse circumstances ; while those who originally branched off from the same root are basking in the sunshine of prosperity—let us ask of our own hearts, whether we should not sometimes feel it hard to be shut out from their indulgences, and thrust down as it were into a lower grade of society altogether, without any fault of our own.

Nor is it so much the fact itself, as the accompaniments of this fact, which we should feel it hard to bear—the willingness of our relations to forget us—their cold or forced civilities when we claimed their attention, compared with the warmth of their emotions towards those who were more distinguished than ourselves—the situations they might point out to us as eligible, but which they would almost die rather than occupy—the times they would choose for inviting us, when no one else was likely to appear—the multitude of things reserved for us to do, when our health required that we should have perfect rest—all which are perfectly natural, and might easily occur without any accompaniment of unkind feeling. Yet, these are only small items of a vast sum, like grains of dust in the long wearisome and humiliating path, which the poor relation must tread in associating with the rich.

In all such circumstances, how much may the facts themselves be ameliorated to the sufferer by the kind and cordial treatment of the mistress of a family, and especially by one whose high sense of justice and generosity admits of no half welcomes beneath her roof! Such a mistress will consider the poor relative as peculiarly under her protection, to guard from slights, to bring forward as occasion may invite, to keep back as circumstances may require, and to render comfortable and at ease whatever may occur. And if in the contemplation of this duty, in addition to those already dwelt upon in this chapter, the English wife should fear that her time will be so occupied in thinking of others, as to leave none for thinking of herself, she must remember, that by these means she will gather around her a strong phalanx of friends, whose love and gratitude will leave her little to wish for, which it is in their power

to supply; and beyond this, she will find that by the same means she has been put in possession of one of the great secrets of human happiness—that of making others happy.

CHAPTER XII.

SOCIAL INFLUENCE.

VISITING, and receiving visits, being regarded by some married women as among the most important avocations of life, it may possibly to such individuals imply an ignorance of the claims of society, when I venture to hint at the probability of this being one of the peculiar temptations against which women in general would do wisely to be on their guard, especially against acquiring a habit of visiting, as a means of escape from the dullness and monotony of their own firesides.

It needs but little acquaintance with domestic duty, to know that there must be something wrong in the home of that woman who is always leaving it; although, on the other hand, few persons would recommend exclusive confinement to the same narrow sphere of thought and action, in which we exist at home. It is good to go out into society sometimes, in order that we may return with the greater relish; but a still more extensive amount of good is derived from what we may learn in mixed society, and sometimes even from the humblest individuals we meet with there.

It must, however, depend much upon ourselves, whether we go out prepared to make visiting a wholesome refreshment to the mind, or a means of collecting and disseminating low ideas with regard to our own affairs, and those of our neighbors. When a married woman goes out intent upon reckoning the cost of the entertainment she partakes of, upon comparing her neighbor's furniture with her own, but especially upon depreciating the excellence of all which falls under her notice, it may safely be said that she would have been better at home; but when she goes out with a desire to extend her kindly feelings towards her fellow-creatures in general, to learn from others, and to impart knowledge in return; or, in other words, to do and receive good in any way that may open, she will seldom have the mortification of returning home weary and dispirited, or wishing she had never gone.

But pleasant as this kind of refreshment may occasionally be, and necessary as it is sometimes to mix with others in order to have our views enlarged, and our prejudices rubbed off, the woman who makes it the chief business of her life to visit and receive company, will have committed a lamentable mistake by getting married; for this business might unquestionably have been carried on in her single state with as much enjoyment to herself, and with far less injury to the happiness of others. Whatever is done by a married woman in the way of duty, must have reference to others, and more especially to those with whom she is most intimately connected; how then can it be promoting their interests, or making their welfare the chief object of desire, for her to be bestowing her time, her intelligence—nay, all that is pleasing in her manners, and interesting in her character, upon comparative strangers; while her lassitude, weariness, and exhaustion, the natural effects of too much excitement, are brought home to her own family, and unsparingly indulged before them.

There are probably few English wives who would really wish to enter at once upon so unnatural a way of living; but there are unfortunately too many, who from want of firmness to resist temptation, as well as prudence and discernment to foresee what consequences must inevitably follow certain acts, are drawn into that vortex of dissipation apparently against their will, and, if one could really believe their protestations, still more decidedly against their inclinations.

There is no more curious phenomenon, presented by human life, than that of innumerable multitudes of persons doing every day, towards each other, with every demonstration of delight, what one half at least of the same individuals declare themselves to be doing with the utmost unwillingness, and even with dislike. In nothing is this more striking than in the ceremony of making morning calls. The devices which are practised to escape from callers, on the one hand, and to call upon persons who are not at home, on the other, might put to shame the warmest advocate for keeping up these forms of polished life. For let the whole nation, as with one stout heart, determine to speak the truth, and say exactly what degree of willingness is really felt to go out and make these calls, or to stay at home and receive them, and let the willingness thus avowed, be made the rule of their future conduct, what an immense amount of precious time would thus be rescued from worse than waste!

Nor is it the absolute calls themselves, which constitute the whole objection to the practice as it is now carried on, for every mistress of a family addicted to this practice, knows that there are two or three good hours—nay, actually the very best of every day, which she can never call her own, and which she consequently makes no attempt to spend in any rational or useful manner. If any thing within the sphere of her duties has really to be done, it must be hurried through between, perhaps, a late breakfast, and the arrival of those few early callers, who come on business, or who really wish to find the lady of the house at home. When these are gone, the first part of the farce commences, and if the after scenes could be made to vary so as to develop what was interesting or new, there would perhaps be less objection to the whole. But, unfortunately, having gone through one set of observations, one series of little surprises at the intelligence of the day, one succession of animated smiles, and expressions of profound interest, no sooner is another guest announced, than the lady of the house has to be just as much astonished at the news, and just as much startled at each item of intelligence, as if she had never heard it before—just as much pleased to receive the twentieth caller as the first, and although in all probability no single truth has been told her with which she was not all the while acquainted, no new idea developed, and no feeling, except weariness, excited, she has to remain until the last as fascinating, vivacious, and apparently delighted, as she was at first.

Now if this is not hard labor, I am ignorant what labor is. If this is not waste of time, I am ignorant what is its use. If this is not a weariness and degradation to the spirit, I am ignorant on that point too. Allowing, however, that calls are necessary, a fact I do not pretend to dispute, allowing also that some particular portion of each day should be appropriated to that purpose, what harm, I would ask, would result to society in general, from having that time compressed into the space of one hour each day. It is true that by this means many callers would probably have to be introduced at the same time, but here would be the great advantage, that the same common-place remarks would do for all at once, the same little starts of astonishment, the same expression of interest lighting up the face, and beyond this, the same delighted welcome for the many, embodied in one, might have a better chance of being really cordial and sincere. In addition to these advantages, every married woman should have the privilege of fixing her own hour as a generally understood thing, so that her household arrangements might be made accordingly; and time comparatively secure would thus be left for pursuing any more important avocations without fear of interruption.

I now appeal to the wives of England, whether the carrying out of such a plan would not be felt as a general relief; more especially since it need only be adopted by those who consider time too precious a gift to be spent in a sort of trifling which seems neither to do good, nor to give satisfaction; while all who prefer the present system, would enjoy the gratification of spending their whole mornings either in making or receiving calls. The only difference to them would be, that they could no longer with any

justice complain of the system as irksome or annoying.

In such observations I would be understood to refer to those calls of ceremony, habit, or fancied necessity, which are universally complained of behind the scenes. Visits of friendship are of a totally different order, and might be arranged for accordingly. But whatever plans may be proposed, the great evil to be avoided is, a universal determination to appear pleased with what is as universally complained of as a waste of time, and a tax upon patience and sincerity; for that can never be a right state of things, where a general grievance is borne with under the pretence of its being a pleasure. There are many grievances which must be borne with, and which it is consequently desirable to make the best of; and there are others which fall heavily upon individuals, and yet conduce to the general good; but that a burden felt by all, and sincerely deplored by the majority of those who bear it, should come not only to be submitted to, but apparently rejoiced in, is a phenomenon which exhibits so striking an instance of the self-mastery of woman, that one cannot sufficiently regret this exercise of her magnanimity not being devoted to a nobler cause.

The art of receiving guests agreeably, arranging them judiciously, and treating them so that every one shall feel perfectly at ease, is of more importance to the mistress of a house, than the display of her richest jewels, or her most studied accomplishments. Indeed, there is always this fact to be borne in mind with regard to society in general, that nothing which is merely an embellishment to ourselves, can, as regards its real value, bear the slightest proportion to that which affords gratification to others. The mistress of a house would do little for the enjoyment of her guests by being the most splendidly dressed, or even the most striking and distinguished person in her own drawing-room. The probability is that half of them would go away secretly, if not openly, affronted. Her proper duty is to allow them an opportunity of shining, if they can; and in pursuance of this subject, she will endeavor to make way for the distinguished, as well as to bring forward the retiring. But more especially it is her part to be unobtrusively watchful of individual comfort, attentive to every wish, moving about from one to another without bustle or officiousness, and above all things taking care that the most insignificant are not neglected. She must do all this too with a perfect knowledge of what is in human nature, so as not to offend while endeavoring to please; and with a perfect adaptation of herself to the different characters of her guests, whose enjoyment for the evening must be in a great measure at her disposal. Thus the mistress of a house may attain the desirable object of having her visitors all pleased and satisfied, without any of them being aware how much of their gratification they owe to her; for I am supposing her one of those unselfish women, who, when they go into company, are intent only upon the happiness of those around them, and who consequently escape the disappointment of having failed in their own persons to be either courted or admired.

But there is a far different manner of visiting and receiving visits from this—and I had almost said, would that there were no other with which we had any thing to do! I mean where one or more friends—real friends, are invited by the mistress of a house to be for a short time the companions of her fireside enjoyments, and, as members of the same family, to partake in whatever may constitute its amusements or its privileges. Here then we find an appropriate and ample field for the full development of those qualifications, whether natural or acquired, which are combined in an agreeable companion; for here are happily united, freedom for the exercise of truth, time for narrative, opportunity for confidence, resource for intellect, occasion for pleasantry, recollections shared together, hopes mutually anticipated, and indeed any thing which an affectionate heart, and an enlightened understanding, can require for enjoyment.

What a luxury too it is for a married woman to feel such perfect identity with her husband in all he is, and in all he possesses, that her home, her books, her garden, seem to be her very own to place at the disposal of her friend; but greater than all, is the luxury of gathering into her bosom that fulness of delight, derived from ten thousand sources, yet all embodied in the simple feeling, that she has a home to offer. There is nothing in the joy of girlhood equal to this; and say what people will about marriage being the grave of friendship, I cannot think the wife is the person most to blame where it is so. Perhaps there is no blame at all, for I should rather think the falling off of female friends might, in a great measure, be attributed to a natural shrinking, on the side of the unmarried party, from admitting, as she supposes he must be, a man, and perhaps a stranger, into her confidence. There are, however, so very few men who care any thing at all about such confidence, who feel any curiosity to know what female friendship is composed of, or who even listen when its details are laid before them, that such an objection need scarcely be allowed to interfere with the freedom of intercourse, which constitutes one of the great privileges of friendship, and without which it must be little better than a name.

Beyond this, too, there may be a little fault on the part of the unmarried friend, in attaching ideas of what is interesting, exclusively to those unfamiliar scenes, and images of impossible perfection, which occupy the mind of the romantic, or the highly imaginative, to the exclusion of what is real, practical, and true. Thus the wife who really does her duty, is not unfrequently condemned by her female friends, as being a commonplace, and perhaps a vulgar, or degenerate being. But could they really know what deep and thrilling interests are to her involved in this her duty, what high and burning zeal—what quenchless ardor—what enthusiasm, what feeling, are expended upon the avocations of each day, marked as they must be, by the ebb and flow of affection's ceaseless tide; could they see all this, how would they start astonished at their own mistake, in having supposed that the mere material elements upon which the duties of a wife were exercised, were in themselves what constituted the reality of all the interest which she had in life. No; beyond these visible signs which tell of the observance or neglect of duty, she has a life—a soul—a spiritual existence, which comprises every thing between the wide extremes of happiness and wo; and if her early associates will not believe it, if they will withdraw themselves, and think, and say, that she is changed, it is because she regards all the intense and profound realities of the life she now leads, as too sacred to be unveiled even before the eye of friendship.

But she is not changed: a warm, true-hearted woman cannot change to those she has loved in early life, simply because her name, her home, and the occupations which fill up her time, are not the same. Affection in such a heart can never die; where it has once fixed, it will retain its hold; and if by force it should be shaken off, it will be like wrenching away a portion of the heart itself. If new ties are formed, it does not follow that the old ones shall be broken. They rather grow into the soul from having been interwoven with its earliest affections, and if they are less observable in after life, it is only because they lie the deepest, and are consequently the most concealed.

But to return to the subject of duty; in the act of entertaining her familiar friends, and particularly those who are younger than herself, the married woman may possibly suppose that she enjoys only a pleasant recreation, by which the more serious business of life may be diversified with social amusement. But however much this might have been the case in her single state, it is so no longer; for as the mistress of a house, and the head of a family, she holds a relation to her young friends which is necessarily invested with a degree of authority, and for the use of this authority she is as a Christian woman accountable. Even if no attempt is made to use her influence, so as to give to the minds around her a bias either one way or another,

some bias will necessarily be given by the general character of her establishment, and the tone of feeling by which her domestic and social affairs are regulated. Besides which, her young friends will naturally look to her to see what plans she wishes to adopt, and what principles it is her object to carry out, and their conduct will be regulated accordingly; for whatever the degree of familiarity may be which exists between them, the rules which she has adopted for the government of her household, they will feel it an obligation strictly to observe.

The mistress of a house too, will have an influence beyond this, and one which is rarely enjoyed through any other medium of communication; for if she be one who has cultivated and embellished her own mind, storing up for the benefit of others all those means of being agreeable which no woman ought to neglect, she will be the delight of her young friends as a fireside companion, and as such will share in all their moments of unrestrained vivacity, and unlimited freedom.

The authority of teachers, and unfortunately sometimes that of parents too, extends only to those hours of discipline which are spent immediately under their care. Could any system of scholastic instruction be made to regulate without spoiling the sports of children, or could any means of influence be made to operate upon their play, what an amount of additional good might be effected in the formation of individual character! For how often is it found that the child who is taught, questioned, and examined by his masters, who answers freely and fluently on the points referred to, and who is ready and prompt as if his whole mind was there, is in reality but an actor performing his part in that august presence, from which, the moment he is dismissed, his real character bursts forth in the play-ground, to be developed in an entire being as opposite to that which stood before the desk, as if they held no relation to each other! How often too, do we find that persons who appear staid and demure on serious occasions, are most objectionable companions in their mirth; while, on the other hand, those whose mirth is innocent and pure, and guiltles sof all taint from selfish or malignant feeling, may safely be trusted when they are in earnest.

But the mistress of a family in the midst of her young friends enjoys the high privilege of giving a right tone to their enjoyments, and chastening the spirit of their mirth. That is, if she has so cultivated her own understanding as to know what belongs to nature, and to be able to adapt herself to it; for without this power, she must ever be a stranger to the inner and more potent workings of the human heart. But if she has studied those accomplishments which are particularly attractive to youth, and those more important qualifications of mind and intellect which give superiority as well as interest wherever they are found, she will be able to render the moments spent beneath her roof the most privileged perhaps of a whole lifetime—moments in which good impressions were rendered indelible as being accompanied by the most delightful associations—moments retained within the richest treasury of memory, to be made the pattern of the choicest intercourse, and the highest intellectual communion through other chains of association, extending onwards from family to family, and from heart to heart, into a never-ending future.

We see here the consequences which I have perhaps sufficiently dwelt upon, of having cultivated the art of being agreeable, not to shine in general society, as is too frequently the case; not to establish any personal claim to admiration, merely to render striking and brilliant the intellectual companionship of a single hour, but to make the fireside circle a centre of attraction to which the young may love to resort; to render home the chosen spot of earth, where all who are admitted within its social fellowship may delight to dwell, where hopes and joys may be shared together, and where all the thoughts most cherished and enjoyed, are such as tend towards a happier and holier state of existence.

Without having studied the cultivation of the mind, or the embellishment of the character in general, how can the mistress of a family throw around the scenes of home-enjoyments this intellectual and spiritual charm? How can she keep away the cloud of dulness, the monotony of common-place, the shadow of discontent, of which young persons so often complain when visiting their married friends? and how, when her intercourse with them is marked by no lively or impressive character, can she expect that her influence over them will extend to what is lasting or good? It is impossible; because it is not in the nature of the human heart to be thus influenced, without being thus impressed.

To the married woman, then, it is a serious thing to have lost, by indolence or neglect, those golden opportunities of being useful to society, which her position naturally places within her reach. For it is not so much our private precepts which have weight, and perhaps still less our public ones, so much as the influence of individual character upon a surrounding circle, and through that circle upon the world at large.

The English wife should, therefore, regard her position as a central one, and remember that from her, as the head of a family, and the mistress of a household, branch off in every direction trains of thought, and tones of feeling, operating upon those more immediately around her, but by no means ceasing there; for each of her domestics, each of her relatives, and each of her familiar friends, will in their turn become the centre of another circle, from which will radiate good or evil influence, extending onwards, in the same manner, to the end of all things—to the disruption of all earthly ties, and the union of the great family of heaven, where sweet and harmonious notes of her own teaching may possibly be numbered with the songs of the blessed forever and forever.

Is it then a subject merely to be glanced over with a careless wish that we could be useful to our fellow-creatures?—that we could leave on the minds of those who will remember us when we are dead, some lasting impress worthy of their high destiny and ours? All may do this. Of that we are convinced. But are we equally or sufficiently convinced that some impress will, and must be left, whether we have desired it or not? And what if it should be such as to mark them out for wrath in the great day of wrath! And if that too should have spread, as the other might have done, on—on—from one circle and one generation to another—from one family, one community, one people, one country, widening on every hand until the world itself should suffer from the universal taint!

The carrying out of such a thought to its full extent is too tremendous, and yet we know of no natural limits by which influence either good or evil can be confined or arrested in its progress towards eternity. We can only ask with penitence and prayer that what we have hitherto exercised amiss may be overruled for good, and that what we have yet to exercise, may be directed by Him who alone can give the power to use it for his glory.

There are many cases of practical duty, in which it seems as if the language of Scripture had, by general consent, been explained away as referring to times and circumstances in which we have no part. In none is this more striking than as regards hospitality, few of us considering ourselves at all the more required from any thing we meet with there, when we prepare a feast, to call in the poor or the friendless to partake. Without pretending to be wiser than others, by applying these and similar injunctions more literally than they appear to be generally understood, it seems to me a question of deep importance to a serious mind, whether we are not many of us required to go much further than we do in extending our hospitality to those who, according to the usages of the world, may appear to have but little claim upon such attentions.

There is an extensive class of persons, who, if we would do to them as we would that others should do to us under similar circumstances, instead of being objects of general neglect, would become objects of our especial kindness in this respect. I mean those who are separated from their own home-connections by becoming assistants in business, or otherwise attached to families in which they are comparatively strangers.

It cannot be denied that a system of hospitality thus carried out towards persons so circumstanced, or according to the Scripture rule of inviting those who cannot ask us in return, would require the exercise of considerable self-denial as well as benevolence; and more especially so with those whose homes are the centre and the source of the greatest happiness they enjoy; for it is perhaps the only disadvantage accompanying an excess of this home-feeling, that the more perfect is the satisfaction with which we gather into the domestic circle, the less willingness we feel that a stranger should " intermeddle with its joys."

Thus we sometimes find a sort of household exclusiveness, and a too great concentration of domestic satisfaction, prevailing almost to the extent of selfishness, where such feelings are indulged without the restraint of judgment or of principle. To persons infected with this home-mania, their own houses, their own grounds, their own habits, and their own modes of thinking and living are always the very best imaginable, and such as bear no comparison with those of any other family. So much is this the case, that they seem almost to be a law unto themselves; while above every thing they reject the idea of being improved by adopting the views and the practices of others. It is needless to say that such persons have little weight to throw into the scale of social influence either on the side of good or evil, for the absurdities they exhibit to the world effectually prevent their doing any considerable amount of harm beyond what is negative.

But there are degrees of this evil against which we may not all be sufficiently on our guard, because we may be mistaking it for good; yet when it stands in the way of our practising the duty of hospitality, we shou'd ask ourselves seriously whether that home which ought to be the scene of our greatest earthly happiness is not in reality the temple of our worship. A higher cultivation of the feelings of kindness and benevolence towards others, a deeper sympathy for their trials and sufferings, a more earnest solicitude for their welfare, and a greater desire to impart the blessings we enjoy, would, I am persuaded, tend very much to reconcile us to any temporary interruption of our domestic enjoyments which might be occasioned by the presence of a stranger, even should his habits and modes of thinking be the most dissimilar to our own. And if any thing could be done by this means to improve the minds and morals of that important class of society who will constitute the next generation of men of business—men who will give the weight of extensive influence either to the side of good, or evil, that strong feeling of household exclusiveness, which is but a refined and extended selfishness, ought certainly in some measure to give way.

We complain of the habits of young men, and with some cause, yet when we recollect of what materials human nature is composed, and compare these with the situation of young men generally; but more especially when we think of the thousand inviting avenues to sin which are opened to their choice, the cordiality with which they are met by evil associates, and invited to every rendezvous of vice; and when we compare this with the very little cordiality they meet with on the opposite side; the scanty welcomes, the cold notice, and the treatment equally distant and disrespectful, we surely must expect them to be more than human wholly to withstand the one, and to bind themselves over with lasting and warm attachment to the other.

Young men, too, are often diffident of their own attractions in polished society, and sometimes not without considerable reason, more especially when they find themselves treated in respectable company with every demonstration of contempt. Here, then, we must also remember that vice is not delicate in her distinctions. In her wide halls of revelry, the ignorant, the mean, and the unlettered find a welcome. She slights them not for want of polished manners. She heeds neither personal inferiority, nor unfashionable attire. All—all are welcome, from the raw stripling, to the friendless stranger, who finds not in the wide world another or a safer home.

In contemplating this view of the subject, I have often thought, what an amount of good might be effected, if a little more attraction were held out by Christians in general, towards persons of this class. We ought seriously to question, too, whether we are really doing them justice—whether we are not resting too well satisfied in merely urging upon them the necessity of attention to public worship, when a few more welcomes into Christian families might possibly do more for their real good, than many sermons without participation in the real comforts of any respectable home.

Nor is it the mere invitation of such persons at stated times, which can effect the good so much required, the mere bestowment of a dinner, or the mere permission to come on Sundays and be present during the hours of family devotion. Good as this unquestionably is, there is something else required; and this something should be supplied by the mistress of the house; for, I repeat, that to woman all the common usages of kindness are so easy and familiar, as to leave her little excuse for neglecting the claims of hospitality, which constitute so essential a part of social duty. There is much kind feeling conveyed even by so slight an act as a cordial shake of the hand, but especially by those apparently slight observations upon personal affairs, which evince an interest in the situation and circumstances of a guest, and which often lead to a freedom of communication which, as a means of influence, may be turned to the happiest account.

In all associations in which the feelings and affections are concerned, it must never be forgotten, that the *manner* in which an act of benevolence is done, is often of far greater importance than the act itself.—That it is possible to be kind in an unkind manner; to give a great deal away, and yet be most ungenerous. This truth we have many of us, at some time or other of our lives, had to feel perhaps too keenly for our peace. Yet it is possible the thought of what such kindness cost us, may prove a wholesome one in its effect upon our own conduct towards others, by teaching us how to soothe, where through ignorance we might have wounded; how to attract, where we might have repelled; and consequently how to do good, where we might inadvertently have done evil.

But it is useless to think of the manner, until we have seen the act itself to be a duty; and I would here appeal to the wives of England, as they value the good of their country, and the good of their sons and brothers—as they value youth in general, and regard it as the season for remembering our Creator, and the Giver of all our blessings—as they would cherish its buoyant hopes, strengthen its high capabilities, and lay an imperishable foundation of good, where evil must otherwise enter and occupy the vacant room—as they value all these considerations, I would urge them not to confine their social kindness merely to those who can requite them after their own manner; but to extend it to those who, though comparatively strangers, share in the affections and the feelings of a common nature, and who are now undergoing the formation of their characters for time and for eternity.

" Not following lower things,"—was a noble motto adopted by a noble queen,* when she chose as emblematical of the course she intended to pursue, a marigold turning to the sun. Although nothing could be more at variance with the duties of a wife, and especially one of that class of society to which this work more especially applies, than to be aspiring after any selfish or personal aggrandizement as regards mere sublunary things; there is an ambition, if I may call it such, which ought to fill the heart, and rouse the energies of every Christian woman who stands at the head of a household, whatever

---

* Marguarite of Valois, sister of Francis I., and Queen of Navarre.

her position may be with regard to outward circumstances. I refer to that aspiration after higher and holier things, which lifts the soul out of its grovelling anxieties and worldly cares, and directs its hopes unchangeably towards the world which is eternal.

It is not consistent with the aim of the writer in such a work as this, to enter fully upon the subject of that change of heart which alone can qualify for forming any just or proper estimate of what belongs to a preparation for the heavenly state. Had such been my intention, I would not have left the consideration of so momentous and sublime a theme, to the last few pages of this work. But leaving this subject, in its vastness and its depth—its absorbing interests, and its solemn truths, to writers of a higher and a weightier character, I would still indulge a hope that what has here been said may in some degree assist towards a more full and satisfactory exemplification of the Christian character. For even where religion is felt and owned to be the one thing needful, and where it is adopted as the principle and the rule of life, those familiar avocations which occupy the attention of every day are not always conducted in the spirit which ought to regulate the Christian's life. Some good persons err on these points from ignorance; some from want of thought, and many from not regarding them as essential to religion; and thus the standard of excellence is lowered, and we come to be " satisfied with inferior things."

It would as ill become me, as it would be contrary to my feelings, to speak in an unkind or censorious spirit of those, who with good intentions, and while making great endeavors, fall short in little things; but I am convinced that along with this deficiency, there is, to a certain extent, a tendency to aim at what is low, sufficient of itself to prevent the attainment of what is great. The more circumscribed our influence, the less this tendency is seen and felt; but when we take the direction of a household, and consequently have much to do with the formation of the characters around us, this tendency to grovel tells to an amazing and incalculable extent.

It is far from my wish to write on this subject as one who has neither knowledge nor feeling of what wives in general have to struggle with, in the way of depressing or degrading circumstances. I know that the occupations of a household, by reminding us perpetually of what is material, have a strong tendency to occupy the mind with that alone. I know that under wasted health, or weariness, or disappointment, to be urged to struggle after what is high, sounds like a mockery to the human heart. And I know too that there are trials in the lot of woman, almost sufficient of themselves to quench the very life within her soul, and to extinguish there the power to hope for any thing before the grave. I know that the spirit may be harassed—wounded—broken ; but I am yet to learn, that under any circumstances we are justified in giving all things up.

I should rather reason thus—that having striven after excellence in every department, we have so multiplied our resources, that something always must be left; so that if nothing in the shape of positive happiness could ever reach us more, we should still be capable of adding to the happiness of others.

But the most powerful and widely prevailing cause of that moral and intellectual degradation—that downward tendency of the mind, and that grovelling of the spirit among material things, which is so much to be lamented over in the wives of the present day, arises clearly and unquestionably out of the false estimate so universally formed of what is most to be desired—nay, of what is absolutely essential to existence. It is this vain and fruitless ambition with regard to worldly things, in which we are all more or less engaged, that wears down our energies, and wearies out our hopes. It is the disappointment, the perplexity, the harass of this long struggle, which leaves us so spiritless and worn. It is the emptiness of our success when the highest worldly wish has been attained, which makes us, in the midst of

all our coveted possessions, so miserably poor.

It is difficult to speak strongly on these subjects, yet with that kindness and respect which I feel that my countrywomen deserve, and deserve especially from me. But when I assert again that it is not intention which is in fault, so much as a certain set of mistaken views which more or less affect us all, I would fondly hope I might obtain their forgiveness for being more than commonly earnest in so important a cause. In this hope I appeal to their own hearts, whether the daily conflict they are many of them enduring is not in reality after that which " perisheth in the using ;" whether it ever brings them a reward at all commensurate with what it costs ; and whether it is not in itself a weariness to the very soul. I appeal to society at large, whether the importance we many of us attach to appearing well before the world, in other words, to dressing and living in a certain style, has not irritated more tempers, destroyed more peace, occasioned more disputes, broken more spirits, crossed more love, hindered more improvement, and caused more spiritual declension, than any other single cause which could be named. And what has it done to throw into the opposite scale? Encouraged one kind of manufactory to the disadvantage of another, changed our fashions, excited our vanity, furnished our houses, decked our persons—and what then! Sent us forth into society envied and envying one another, and disseminating wherever we might go, low thoughts, disparaging allusions, and uncharitable feelings, all arising out of the very rivalry and competition of which this fruitless ambition was the source.

Let us look at one channel only among the many thousands through which it operates to the destruction of human happiness, and the disunion of natural ties. It is no poet's fable, and I speak it reverently, believing what I speak, when I say, that the love which grows up between two young people who expect to spend their lives together, is of every earthly feeling that which most endears to us all which is most excellent in itself, most beautiful in the creation, and most beneficent in the dispensations of an all-wise and eternal God. Who then would quench this feeling, or lower its exercise, or make it a mere slave to wait upon the customs of the world? The voice of humanity exclaims against so base, so foolish a perversion of our nature. Youth exclaims against it, as well it may. Society—the world exclaims. The world? No, that can never be. It is the world whose unrelenting voice demands this sacrifice—the world before whose artificial glare the star of love must hide its purer ray.

It is because the world is the great altar upon which the hearts of multitudes are laid, that the shrine of domestic happiness so often is profaned by broken vows—vows broken in the spirit, and therefore the mere symbols of a love, without its sweetness or its life. It is because the spirit of the world demands that we should love and serve the mammon of unrighteousness, that hearts are bought and sold, and youth is wedded to old age, and every mockery of feeling which imagination can conceive, is perpetrated under the grave name of prudence. I have myself advocated prudence, and I have urged the necessity of waiting for what are popularly considered as sufficient means. Yet this has been chiefly in conformity with the universal system we acknowledge, of "regarding lower things." I did not, and I never shall, believe the system is a right one in itself; but until our views are more enlightened, and our principles are strong enough to support us in the effort, it would be worse than folly to advise that individuals here and there should overstep the bounds of prudence as they are now laid down, not knowing what they did.

The new order of things which I would advocate must be a general one, brought about by simultaneous views, and feelings, and determinations. There will then be no world to fear, for we shall constitute ourselves a world, in which lower things will no longer be regarded, except as such—a world in which the warmest feelings of the heart will no longer be considered as bearing any com-parison, in value, with the cold formalities of artificial life—a world in which what we wear, and what we use, shall no longer be esteemed as more important than what we do—a world in which people shall be judged of by what they are, and not by what they possess—a world in which what is costly and brilliant in ornament, shall give place to that which is excellent in character, and sterling in value.

And when shall this bright epoch arrive?—this dawning of better hopes—this day of promise for our country, and our homes? It will arrive when the wives of England shall hold themselves above their circumstances; and, estimating that most highly which is really high, shall understand how principle is the basis of all good; and having subjected these principles to the word of God, and tried them by the only test which is safe and true, they may then adorn the superstructure by all which the purest taste and the most chastened feeling can suggest.

In adopting the motto of one of the most amiable and accomplished of female sovereigns, we must not forget that hers was the pursuit of excellence of almost every kind; in her studies, her attainments, and in all those graces of mind and person which adorn a court. Nor do I see why the raising of our highest admiration to that which is highest in itself, should in any respect interfere with our desire after excellence in general.

It is a melancholy thought, when marriage has united the destiny of two human beings for this life at least, that one of them should grow indifferent to those qualities of mind and person which formed the chief attraction to the other. It is a melancholy thought, that when a wife has taken upon herself the du-ties which belong to the mistress of a family, she should be willing to lose those charms which constitute the loveliness of woman. It is a melancholy thought, that because she has become a useful, she must cease to be an in-tellectual, being. But it cannot—it must not be. The very thought is one of treason against the love and the happiness of mar-ried life; for what is there among all the embellishments of female character, which this love cannot legitimately appropriate, and this happiness enhance and improve?

In no other situation in life can woman find so appropriate a sphere for the exercise of every grace, and the display of every charm, as in the centre of her home-enjoyments; yet here, how often do we find that she permits all the poetry of her mind to be extinguished, and after that the beautiful too often fades away. Life may remain the same to her in all its tangible realities; but as the sunshine passes from the landscape, so the light which gives freshness and vividness to every object, is gone forever.

It is said she has actual and pressing cares, which absorb her attention, to the exclusion of other, and especially of higher, thoughts. But here again is her mistake. It is not in woman's nature to be degraded or brought down by care, provided only the objects of her solicitude are worthy in themselves, or such as call forth feelings worthy of being indulged. The care—the love—the brooding tenderness of a fond mother or a faithful wife—when, I would ask, was woman found the worse for these? No. It is the element in which she lives, to care for those she loves. It is in this element that all her virtues rise and shine; while her whole character assumes a higher and more spiritual excellence. We talk of altered circumstances, and personal privations, but we libel the true heart of woman when we think it cannot stand the shock of such extremes as these. No, these are not the foes she fears; and it is an insult to her understanding, when society persuades her that she does fear them. Within her heart of hearts she has a nobler conviction, that her husband's happiness, and her own integrity and truth, are more to her than all the riches in the world. Why then, with these convictions, and with that strong capability which constitutes her dower, of rising above the tide of circumstance, and living apart from worldly things in the higher world of her affections—why will woman stoop to be the slave of habit, of custom, and most of all, of fashion, until her vanity and self-indul-

gence become the bane of man's existence, and her own?

And is it well that men, whose daily avocations necessarily call into service, as one of their great principles of action, a worldly and a selfish spirit—is it right that they should be urged, nay, goaded on, in the perpetual race of personal and family aggrandizement, by those who profess to love them, and who, consequently, ought to seek their ultimate and real good? May we not rather leave to them the whole adjustment of these worldly matters? It is their business, and their duty, to find a place among their fellow-men, to establish a footing in society, and to maintain it by all just and honorable means. This is no care of woman's. Her appropriate part is to adorn that station wherever it may be, by a contented mind, an enlightened intellect, a chastened spirit, and an exemplary life.

I have dwelt much upon the influence of woman in social and domestic life, and in her married state she will find that influence extending almost on every hand. What, then, will be her situation, without the aid of personal religion, to give a right direction to its operations upon other minds? But what will be her situation altogether without this aid?

The thought is too appalling.

> "A boat sent out to sail alone
> At midnight on the moonless sea,"

might bear some comparison to the situation of a solitary being trusting herself upon the world's great ocean without this guide; but a richly-freighted vessel, crowded with human beings, and bearing in its bosom the interests of as many souls, yet venturing out to sea without a pilot, without a compass, without any hope or means of safety, might with more justice be compared to the woman who should dare to engage in the deep responsibilities of married life, without religion to direct her course. Whatever difficulties may be thus encountered, she cannot meet them alone. Whatever dangers, others are drawn in to share them with her. Whatever storms, she braves them only at the peril of the precious lives committed to her trust. Whatever rock she strikes upon, it wrecks not her alone, but all—all the rich treasury of hopes and interests which she bore along with her in that presumptuous course, and for all these she is accountable. I repeat, the thought is too appalling. Let us turn to scenes of more familiar occurrence, where there is more satisfaction, because there is more hope.

There is a large class of persons, who without having given up their hearts entirely to the influence of personal religion, are wishing that they could do so, and intending some time or other that they will. On all solemn occasions they feel as if they actually would; and never more so perhaps than when they enter upon the duties of married life. To woman this is so great and important a change, that it naturally produces, if any thing can, trains of reflection highly favorable to an altered and improved state of mind altogether; and if she has ever seriously thought of religion, she does so then. Those who rest satisfied with good intentions, and especially in religious matters, are glad of any alteration in their circumstances which they think will make it easier to begin; and they hail the opening of a new life, as the entrance upon one which will be more exemplary than the past. Thus it is often with perfect sincerity, that the young religious professor believes she will set out upon a new career when engaging in the duties of a wife. Her feelings are much softened, too, by separation from her former friends; she fears the difficulties of her untried path; and thus is altogether more disposed than ever in her life before to do, and to be, what she sees clearly to be right. If, under these circumstances, she has married a good man, her first temptation will be to think, for that reason, that she must be good herself; if a man who has little or no religion, her first trial will be to find that instead of being helped, as she had expected, so smoothly on her way, she has, in addition to her own difficulties, to help him and all his household.

But a more familiar temptation, and a more frequent trial than either of these, is one which steals by its insidious nature into the very heart of domestic life; and it works the more deceitfully by mixing itself up with all that is most reputable and most approved in society in general, and not less than others, in the society of the good.

Persons of this description, in all probability, seek the acquaintance of the well-meaning young wife, or she seeks theirs; and being a sincere and somewhat hopeful character, not having much foundation of her own, but easily led on by others, she is induced by their companionship to take a higher standing in religious matters than she ever did before. Encouraged by their kindness, she advances step by step, progressing outwardly, and gaining confidence as she goes on. All this perhaps might be well, for she is still sincere so far as her self-knowledge extends; but here again the spirit of the world creeps in. Indeed the question is, whether she has not all the while been actuated by the spirit of the world, for it is now so reputable to be religious, that temptation can assume this form as well as any other.

With this advance in an outward, and, perhaps, too visible profession, the cares of the young wife increase. The circle of her acquaintance widens. Visits und morning-calls are not to be neglected; and well if they are not devoted to that most objectionable of all kinds of gossip, which chooses the minister and the observances of a religious life, for its theme. But in addition to this, the young wife listens to the popular and common talk about low worldly things. She learns to think much of her furniture, much of her dress, and much of the manner in which she entertains her friends. Nay, she is even glad to see that all this competition does not appear to be discarded from the fashionable world. As time passes on, she becomes more and more absorbed by the growing cares and thickening perplexities of every day; until at last it might become a matter of doubt to those around her, which in reality occupied her thoughts the most, the preparation for a party, or the preparation for eternity.

Need we wonder that such a woman has little religious influence? That she fails to adorn the doctrine of our Saviour, or to commend the faith which she professes? Need we wonder that her husband, her servants, society at large, are not made better by her conversation and her example? Yet strange to say, it is sometimes wondered at that the religious conversation of such persons does not do good, and they themselves, when they have leisure for it, will labor diligently for the conversion of the poor. But they forget that those around them, and especially the poor, are quick-sighted to their inconsistencies, and that they know by other evidence than words, when the world is really in the heart.

By this slight picture, far be it from me to convey an idea that I could represent the really changed in heart; for I know that theirs is a foundation which none of these things move. I speak of those who have been only *almost* persuaded, and who, on the solemn occasion of their marriage, have set out in life with serious views and good intentions; yet whatever may be the clearness of these views, or the strength of these intentions, I believe that a great number of hopeful beginnings have been frustrated by this single root of evil, this spirit of the world. I believe also, that more spiritual declension among women may be traced to the same cause, than to all the vice and all the infidelity to be met with among the openly profane.

It is then against this single enemy, above all others, that married women have to sustain each other in waging constant and determined war. I repeat, it is hard, too hard, for any single individual to struggle against the tide of popular feeling, more especially when religion numbers in her ranks so many who divide her claims with those of the world. But if the happiness of home be precious, we have that at stake. If our intellectual and moral good be worth preserving, we have that to cherish. If our religious influence be the most important treasure committed to our trust, we have that to hold secure. All to which the best feelings of the heart attach themselves as lovely and enduring is ours, if we maintain this conflict as we ought; and sink under it we never need, for we know to whom to go for help.

Let us then remember that a worldly spirit is the very opposite of that which finds its home in Heaven; and if our interests are sufficiently engaged in what is spiritual and eternal, we shall not easily be turned away to fix them upon " lower things."

CPSIA information can be obtained at www.ICGtesting.com
Printed in the USA
BVOW012351150513

320859BV00012B/221/P